Solicitors' Accounts Manual

14TH EDITION

Other titles available from Law Society Publishing:

COFAs Toolkit
Jeremy Black and Florence Perret du Cray

COLPs Toolkit (2nd edn)
Michelle Garlick

Solicitors and the Accounts Rules (3rd edn)
Peter Camp

The Solicitor's Handbook 2017
Andrew Hopper QC and Gregory Treverton-Jones QC

SRA Handbook
Solicitors Regulation Authority

Titles from Law Society Publishing can be ordered from all good bookshops or direct (telephone 0370 850 1422, email **lawsociety@prolog.uk.com** or visit our online shop at **www.lawsociety.org.uk/bookshop**).

SOLICITORS' ACCOUNTS MANUAL

14TH EDITION

Solicitors Regulation Authority

The Law Society

ISBN: 978-1-78446-056-3

1st edition 1986
2nd edition 1987
3rd edition 1990
4th edition 1992
5th edition 1994
6th edition 1996
7th edition 1999
8th edition 2001
9th edition 2004
10th edition 2008
11th edition 2009
12th edition 2011
13th edition 2015

This 14th edition published in 2016 by the Law Society
113 Chancery Lane, London WC2A 1PL

Typeset by Columns Design XML Ltd, Reading
Printed by TJ International Ltd, Padstow, Cornwall

FSC
www.fsc.org
MIX
Paper from responsible sources
FSC® C013056

The paper used for the text pages of this book is FSC certified. FSC (the Forest Stewardship Council) is an international network to promote responsible management of the world's forests.

Contents

Preface

INTRODUCTION

This is the 14th edition of the *Solicitors' Accounts Manual*. It contains a summary of the professional requirements in relation to the handling of client money.

The form and content of the SRA Accounts Rules 2011 (Accounts Rules) remain essentially the same, although some significant changes have been made since the rules took effect on 6 October 2011.

The Accounts Rules are contained in **Part 1** of this Manual and state the position as at 1 November 2016. Parts 1–6 of the Accounts Rules apply to practice carried on from an office in England and Wales. Part 7 no longer applies to practice carried on from an office outside England and Wales, but continues to apply to the practice of a registered European lawyer from an office in England and Wales of an exempt European practice. (The accounts provisions for overseas practice are now contained in the SRA Overseas Rules 2013.)

The contents page lists each rule and its subject matter but readers can also look at the index.

Part 2 of the Manual sets out the SRA Principles 2011, extracts from the SRA Code of Conduct 2011 relevant to the keeping of accounts and the SRA Overseas Practice Rules 2013. **Part 3** contains extracts from the SRA Glossary 2012 relevant to the Accounts Rules. **Parts 4–7** contain an extended range of annexes intended to provide additional information and assistance in complying with the Accounts Rules.

The Accounts Rules and Code of Conduct form part of the SRA Handbook, which is updated periodically as changes are made by the Solicitors Regulation Authority (SRA). The full text of the SRA Handbook and release notes summarising any changes can be found on the SRA's website at **www.sra.org.uk**.

Changes to the Accounts Rules since 2015

Accountant's report

The SRA Accounts Rules 2011 have been amended since April 2015 to take into account changes to requirements around accountants' reports. The changes include:

- the exemption of some firms from the requirement to obtain an accountant's report; and
- the removal of prescriptive test procedures to allow accountants to exercise their professional judgement and concentrate on risks to client money.

There are some transitional arrangements for accountants' reports. For an accounting period ending before 1 November 2015, version 14 of the Accounts Rules still applies. The accountant has to continue to use the checklist (Appendix 4 of version 14) and the old AR1 form of report (Appendix 5 of version 14).

For an accounting period ending on or after 1 November 2015, version 15 of the SRA Accounts Rules is used (there were no accounts rules changes in versions 16–18). The reporting accountant uses a simpler form of report (the new AR1 is included here at Appendix 5 within **Part 1**), and should also refer to the SRA guidance on completing the new annual accountant's report (see Part 6 at **6.4**).

Overseas accounting requirements

There has also been a simplification of the overseas accounting requirements, set out in Part 3 of the SRA Overseas Rules 2013 since publication of version 15 of the SRA Handbook on 1 November 2015. The SRA Overseas Rules 2013 do not require firms to obtain or deliver an accountant's report (including a final report), unless required to do so by the SRA (see **Part 2** of the Manual at **2.3**).

Since publication of version 15 of the SRA Handbook on 1 November 2015, the accounts rules for overseas practice have been set out in Part 3 of the SRA Overseas Rules 2013. (The accounts provisions applying to the practice of a registered European lawyer from an office in England and Wales of an exempt European practice remain in Part 7 of the SRA Accounts Rules 2011.)

Transitional arrangements for overseas practice mean that firms with an accounting period end date before 1 November 2015 must comply with rule 2C.1 of the SRA Overseas Rules 2013 in all dealings with client money (overseas), but follow the requirements for accountants' reports in version 14 of the SRA Accounts Rules 2011 (see **www.sra.org.uk**). These firms must therefore obtain and deliver the form of report for overseas practice (AR2), including a final report if appropriate.

Possible future changes

The SRA has recently consulted on its plans to review the Accounts Rules in their entirety, and proposes to:

- **Simplify the Accounts Rules:** by focusing on key principles and requirements for keeping client money safe, including:

- keeping client money separate from firm money;
- ensuring client money is returned promptly at the end of a matter;
- using client money only for its intended purpose;
- proportionate requirements for firms to obtain an annual accountant's report.

It is anticipated that the Accounts Rules will be significantly shorter and will be supported by an online toolkit which will include guidance and case studies to aid compliance.

- **Change the definition of client money:** to allow money paid for all fees and disbursements for which the solicitor is liable (for example, counsel's fees) to be treated as the firm's money. Money held for payments for which the client is liable, such as stamp duty land tax, will continue to be treated as client money and therefore required to be held in client account. The impact of the proposed change in definition is expected to remove the need to have a client account for some firms and therefore reduce the associated compliance costs. The changes may also reduce the number of firms required to obtain an accountant's report through the subsequent reduction in the client account balance.
- **Provide an alternative to the holding of client money:** through the introduction of clear and consistent safeguards around the use of third party managed accounts as a mechanism for managing payments and transactions.

The SRA consultation ended 21 September 2016, but it is not thought that any significant changes to the Accounts Rules will become effective until late 2017 although spring 2018 is more likely.

ANNEXES

This edition of the Manual continues to include a range of annexes which are intended to provide additional information and assistance in complying with the rules relating to the handling of client money. The annexes are included in four sections as follows:

- **Part 4:** Holding client money and accounting to clients
- **Part 5:** Charging clients and paying tax
- **Part 6:** Compliance
- **Part 7:** Further sources of information and support

A number of extracts from Law Society practice notes are included (the full text and any future updates can be seen on the Law Society's website at **www.lawsociety.org.uk**). Practice notes represent the Law Society's view of good practice in a particular area and do not constitute legal advice, nor necessarily provide a defence to complaints of misconduct. They use the following terms:

must – refers to a specific legislative requirement or mandatory provision in the SRA Handbook;
should – refers to the Society's view of good practice for most situations outside the regulatory context, and also to any non-mandatory provision in the SRA Handbook;
may – refers to a non-exhaustive list of options for meeting a firm's obligations or running its practice.

The statutory provisions to protect the client accounts of firms, other than licensed bodies, are set out at **4.1**, and those applicable to licensed bodies at **4.2**. The SRA's guidance on dealing with residual client balances, including suggested ways of tracing clients, appears at **4.4**. An SRA warning notice and case studies on using a client account as a banking facility remain at **4.5** and **4.6**, as the improper use of client account is a high risk area of concern (the warning notice contains useful sections on the related issues of holding funds "in escrow" and private client services). There is also a new SRA warning notice on missing money from a client account at **4.7** and a new Law Society practice note on the protection of client accounts at **4.8**.

Part 5 includes information on publicising charges, including disbursements, generally, and an annex specifically on charging for telegraphic transfer fees (**5.2**). Extracts from the Law Society's practice note in relation to VAT on counsel's fees remain, along with HMRC's current guidance on tax on bank and building society interest.

Part 6 will be of interest to compliance officers for finance and administration (COFAs), as it contains information on the role of the COFA, and case studies on recording and reporting breaches. It also now includes the SRA Ethics guidance on completing the new annual accountant's report, and on the exemptions from obtaining a report, at **6.4**.

Contact details and some useful publications are listed in **Part 7**.

The Law Society would like to thank Angela Doran for her work in helping to edit this edition of the Manual.

November 2016

[1] Accounts Rules

[1.1] SRA Accounts Rules 2011

[Last updated 12 August 2016]

PREAMBLE

Authority: made by the Solicitors Regulation Authority Board under sections 32, 33A, 34, 37, 79 and 80 of the Solicitors Act 1974, section 9 of the Administration of Justice Act 1985, section 83(5)(h) of, and paragraph 20 of Schedule 11 to, the Legal Services Act 2007 with the approval of the Legal Services Board;

date: 6 October 2011;

replacing: the Solicitors' Accounts Rules 1998;

regulating: the accounts of solicitors and their employees, registered European lawyers and their employees, registered foreign lawyers, recognised bodies and their managers and employees, and licensed bodies and their managers and employees, in respect of practice in England and Wales.

For the definition of words in italics see rule 2 – Interpretation.

INTRODUCTION

The Principles set out in the Handbook apply to all aspects of practice, including the handling of client money. Those which are particularly relevant to these rules are that you must:

- protect client money and assets;
- act with integrity;
- behave in a way that maintains the trust the public places in you and in the provision of legal services;
- comply with your legal and regulatory obligations and deal with your regulators and ombudsmen in an open, timely and co-operative manner; and
- run your business or carry out your role in the business effectively and in accordance with proper governance and sound financial and risk management principles.

The desired outcomes which apply to these rules are that:

- client money is safe;
- clients and the public have confidence that client money held by firms will be safe;
- firms are managed in such a way, and with appropriate systems and procedures in place, so as to safeguard client money;
- client accounts are used for appropriate purposes only; and

- the SRA is aware of issues in a firm relevant to the protection of client money.

Underlying principles which are specific to the accounts rules are set out in rule 1 below.

These rules apply to all those who carry on or work in a firm and to the firm itself (see rules 4 and 5). In relation to a multi-disciplinary practice, the rules apply only in respect of those activities for which the practice is regulated by the SRA, and are concerned only with money handled by the practice which relates to those regulated activities.

PART 1: GENERAL

Rule 1: The overarching objective and underlying principles

1.1 The purpose of these rules is to keep *client money* safe. This aim must always be borne in mind in the application of these rules.

1.2 *You* must comply with the Principles set out in the Handbook, and the outcomes in Chapter 7 of the *SRA Code of Conduct* in relation to the effective financial management of the *firm*, and in particular must:

(a) keep other people's money separate from money belonging to *you* or *your firm*;

(b) keep other people's money safely in a *bank* or *building society* account identifiable as a *client account* (except when the rules specifically provide otherwise);

(c) use each *client's* money for that *client's* matters only;

(d) use money held as *trustee* of a *trust* for the purposes of that *trust* only;

(e) establish and maintain proper accounting systems, and proper internal controls over those systems, to ensure compliance with the rules;

(f) keep proper accounting records to show accurately the position with regard to the money held for each *client* and *trust*;

(g) account for *interest* on other people's money in accordance with the rules;

(h) co-operate with the *SRA* in checking compliance with the rules; and

(i) deliver annual accountants' reports as required by the rules.

Rule 2: Interpretation

2.1 The guidance notes do not form part of the rules.

2.2 The SRA Handbook Glossary 2012 shall apply and, unless the context otherwise requires:

(a) all italicised terms shall be defined; and

(b) all terms shall be interpreted,

in accordance with the *Glossary*.

2.3 References to the Legal Aid Agency are to be read, where appropriate, as including the Legal Services Commission.

Guidance notes

(i) The effect of the definition of "you" is that the rules apply equally to all those who carry on or work in a firm and to the firm itself. See also rule 4 (persons governed by the rules) and rule 5 (persons exempt from the rules).

(ii) The general definition of "office account" is wide. However, rule 17.1(b) (receipt and transfer of costs) and rule 19.1(b) and 19.2(b) (payments from the Legal Aid Agency) specify that certain money is to be placed in an office account at a bank or building society. Out-of-scope money can be held in an office account (which could be an account regulated by another regulator); it must not be held in a client account.

(iii) For a flowchart summarising the effect of the rules, see Appendix 1. For more details of the treatment of different types of money, see the chart "Special situations – what applies" at Appendix 2. These two appendices do not form part of the rules but are included to help solicitors and their staff find their way about the rules.

Rule 3: Geographical scope

3.1 Parts 1 to 6 of these rules apply to practice carried on from an office in England and Wales. Part 7 of these rules applies to the practice of an *REL* from an office in England and Wales of an *Exempt European Practice.*

Rule 4: Persons governed by the rules

4.1 Save as provided in rule 4.2 below, Parts 1 to 6 of these rules apply to *you.*

4.2 In relation to an *MDP*, the rules apply to *you* only in respect of your *regulated activities.*

4.3 Part 6 of the rules (accountants' reports) also applies to reporting accountants.

4.4 If *you* have held or received *client money*, but no longer do so, whether or not *you* continue in practice, *you* continue to be bound by some of the rules.

Guidance notes

(i) "You" is defined in the Glossary. All employees of a recognised body or licensed body are directly subject to the rules, following changes made by the Legal Services Act 2007. All employees in a recognised sole practice are also directly subject to the rules under section 34A of the Solicitors Act 1974. Non-compliance by any member of staff will also lead to the principals being in breach of the rules – see rule 6. Misconduct by an employee can also lead to an order of the SRA or the Solicitors Disciplinary Tribunal under section 43 of the Solicitors Act 1974 imposing restrictions on his or her employment.

(ii) Rules which continue to apply to you where you no longer hold client money include:

(a) rule 7 (duty to remedy breaches);

(b) rule 17.2 and 17.8, rule 29.15 to 29.24 and rule 30 (retention of records);

(c) rule 31 (production of documents, information and explanations);

(d) Part 6 (accountants' reports), and in particular rule 32A and rule 33.5 (delivery of final report), and rule 35.2.

(iii) The rules do not cover trusteeships carried on in a purely personal capacity outside any legal practice. It will normally be clear from the terms of the appointment whether you are being appointed in a purely personal capacity or in your professional capacity. If you are charging for the work, it is clearly being done in a professional capacity. Use of professional stationery may also indicate that the work is being done in a professional capacity.

(iv) A solicitor who wishes to retire from private practice will need to make a decision about any professional trusteeship. There are three possibilities:

(a) continue to act as a professional trustee (as evidenced by, for instance, charging for work done, or by continuing to use the title "solicitor" in connection with the trust). In this case, the solicitor must continue to hold a practising certificate, and money subject to the trust must continue to be dealt with in accordance with the rules.

(b) continue to act as trustee, but in a purely personal capacity. In this case, the solicitor must stop charging for the work, and must not be held out as a solicitor (unless this is qualified by words such as "non-practising" or "retired") in connection with the trust.

(c) cease to be a trustee.

(v) A licensed body may undertake a range of services, comprising both "traditional" legal services and other, related, services of a non-legal nature, for example, where a solicitor, estate agent and surveyor set up in practice together. Where a licensed body practises in this way (an MDP), only some of the services it provides (reserved and other legal activities, and other activities which are subject to one or more conditions on the body's licence) are within the regulatory reach of the SRA. Other, "non-legal", activities of the licensed body may be regulated by another regulator, and some activities may not fall within the regulatory ambit of any regulator.

Rule 5: Persons exempt from the rules

5.1 The rules do not apply to *you* when:

(a) practising as an employee of:

(i) a *local authority*;

(ii) *statutory undertakers*;

(iii) a body whose accounts are audited by the Comptroller and Auditor General;

(iv) the Duchy of Lancaster;

(v) the Duchy of Cornwall; or

(vi) the Church Commissioners; or

(b) practising as the Solicitor of the City of London; or

(c) carrying out the functions of:

(i) a coroner or other judicial office; or

(ii) a sheriff or under-sheriff; or

(d) practising as a *manager* or employee of an *authorised non-SRA firm*, and acting within the scope of that *firm's* authorisation to practise.

Guidance note

(i) A person practising as a manager or employee of an authorised non-SRA firm is exempt from the Accounts Rules when acting within the scope of the firm's authorisation. Thus if a solicitor is a partner or employee in a firm authorised by the Council for Licensed Conveyancers, the rules will not apply to any money received by the solicitor in connection with conveyancing work. However if the solicitor does in-house litigation work – say collecting money owed to the firm – the Accounts Rules will apply to any money received by the solicitor in that context. This is because, whilst in-house litigation work is within the scope of the solicitor's authorisation as an individual, it is outside the scope of authorisation of the firm.

Rule 6: Principals' responsibility for compliance

6.1 All the *principals* in a *firm* must ensure compliance with the rules by the *principals* themselves and by everyone employed in the *firm*. This duty also extends to the *directors* of a *recognised body* or *licensed body* which is a *company*, or to the members of a *recognised body* or *licensed body* which is an *LLP*. It also extends to the *COFA* of a *firm* (whether a *manager* or non-*manager*).

Guidance note

(i) Rule 8.5(d) of the SRA Authorisation Rules requires all firms to have a COFA. The appointment of a COFA satisfies the requirement under section 92 of the Legal Services Act 2007 for a licensed body to appoint a Head of Finance and Administration. Under rule 6 of the accounts rules, the COFA must ensure compliance with the accounts rules. This obligation is in addition to, not instead of, the duty of all the principals to ensure compliance (the COFA may be subject to this duty both as COFA and as a principal). Under rule 8.5(e) of the SRA Authorisation Rules, the COFA of a licensed body must report any breaches, and the COFA of a recognised body must report material breaches, of the accounts rules to the SRA as soon as reasonably practicable. The COFA of a recognised sole practice has a duty to report material breaches under Rule 8.5(e) of the SRA Authorisation Rules. All COFAs must record any breaches and make those records available to the SRA on request. (See also outcomes 10.3 and 10.4 of Chapter 10 of the SRA Code of Conduct in relation to the general duty to report serious financial difficulty or serious misconduct.)

Rule 7: Duty to remedy breaches

7.1 Any breach of the rules must be remedied promptly upon discovery. This includes the replacement of any money improperly withheld or withdrawn from a *client account*.

7.2 In a private practice, the duty to remedy breaches rests not only on the person causing the breach, but also on all the *principals* in the *firm*. This duty extends to replacing missing *client money* from the *principals'* own resources, even if the money has been misappropriated by an employee or another *principal*, and whether or not a claim is subsequently made on the *firm's* insurance or the Compensation Fund.

Rule 8: Liquidators, trustees in bankruptcy, Court of Protection deputies and trustees of occupational pension schemes

8.1 If in the course of practice *you* act as:

(a) a liquidator,

(b) a trustee in bankruptcy,

(c) a *Court of Protection deputy*, or

(d) a trustee of an occupational pension scheme which is subject to section 47(1)(a) of the Pensions Act 1995 (appointment of an auditor) and section 49(1) (separate bank account) and regulations under section 49(2)(b) (books and records),

you must comply with:

(i) the appropriate statutory rules or regulations;

(ii) the Principles referred to, and the underlying principles set out, in rule 1; and

(iii) the requirements of rule 8.2 to 8.4 below;

and will then be deemed to have satisfactorily complied with the Accounts Rules.

8.2 In respect of any records kept under the appropriate statutory rules, there must also be compliance with:

(a) rule 29.15 – bills and notifications of costs;

(b) rule 29.17(c) – retention of records;

(c) rule 29.20 – centrally kept records;

(d) rule 31 – production of documents, information and explanations; and

(e) rule 43A.1 – reporting accountant to check compliance.

8.3 If a liquidator or trustee in bankruptcy uses any of the *firm's client accounts* for holding money pending transfer to the Insolvency Services Account or to a local bank account authorised by the Secretary of State, he or she must comply with the Accounts Rules in all respects whilst the money is held in the *client account*.

8.4 If the appropriate statutory rules or regulations do not govern the holding or receipt of *client money* in a particular situation (for example, money below a certain limit), *you* must comply with the Accounts Rules in all respects in relation to that money.

Guidance notes

(i) The Insolvency Regulations 1994 (S.I. 1994 no. 2507) regulate liquidators and trustees in bankruptcy.

(ii) The Court of Protection Rules 2007 (S.I. 2007 no. 1744 (L.12)) regulate Court of Protection deputies.

(iii) Money held or received by liquidators, trustees in bankruptcy, Court of Protection deputies and trustees of occupational pension schemes is client money but, because of the statutory rules and rule 8.1, it will not normally be kept in a client account. If for any reason it is held in a client account, the Accounts Rules apply to that money for the time it is so held (see rule 8.3 and 8.4).

Rule 9: Joint accounts

9.1 If, when acting in a *client's* matter, *you* hold or receive money jointly with the *client*, another practice or another third party, the rules in general do not apply, but the following must be complied with:

(a) rule 29.11 – statements from banks, building societies and other financial institutions;

(b) rule 29.15 – bills and notifications of costs;

(c) rule 29.17(b)(ii) – retention of statements and passbooks;

(d) rule 29.21 – centrally kept records;

(e) rule 31 – production of documents, information and explanations; and

(f) rule 43A.1 – reporting accountant to check compliance.

A joint account is not a *client account* but money held in a joint account is *client money*.

Operation of the joint account by you only

9.2 If the joint account is operated only by *you*, *you* must ensure that *you* receive the statements from the *bank*, *building society* or other financial institution in accordance with rule 29.11, and have possession of any passbooks.

Shared operation of the joint account

9.3 If *you* share the operation of the joint account with the *client*, another practice or another third party, *you* must:

(a) ensure that *you* receive the statements or duplicate statements from the *bank*, *building society* or other financial institution in accordance with rule 29.11, and retain them in accordance with rule 29.17(b)(ii); and

(b) ensure that *you* either have possession of any passbooks, or take copies of the passbook entries before handing any passbook to the other signatory, and retain them in accordance with rule 29.17(b)(ii).

Operation of the joint account by the other account holder

9.4 If the joint account is operated solely by the other account holder, *you* must ensure that *you* receive the statements or duplicate statements from the *bank*, *building society* or other financial institution in accordance with rule 29.11, and retain them in accordance with rule 29.17(b)(ii).

Rule 10: Operation of a client's own account

10.1 If, in the course of practice, *you* operate a *client's* own account as signatory (for example, as donee under a power of attorney), the rules in general do not apply, but the following must be complied with:

(a) rule 30.1 to 30.4 – accounting records for clients' own accounts;

(b) rule 31 – production of documents, information and explanations; and

(c) rule 43A.1 – reporting accountant to check compliance.

Operation by you only

10.2 If the account is operated by *you* only, *you* must ensure that *you* receive the statements from the *bank*, *building society* or other financial institution in accordance with rule 30, and have possession of any passbooks.

Shared operation of the account

10.3 If *you* share the operation of the account with the *client* or a co-attorney outside *your firm*, *you* must:

(a) ensure that *you* receive the statements or duplicate statements from the *bank*, *building society* or other financial institution and retain them in accordance with rule 30.1 to 30.4; and

(b) ensure that *you* either have possession of any passbooks, or take copies of the passbook entries before handing any passbook to the *client* or co-attorney, and retain them in accordance with rule 30.1 to 30.4.

Operation of the account for a limited purpose

10.4 If *you* are given authority (whether as attorney or otherwise) to operate the account for a limited purpose only, such as the taking up of a share rights issue during the *client's* temporary absence, *you* need not receive statements or possess passbooks, provided that *you* retain details of all cheques drawn or paid in, and retain copies of all passbook entries, relating to the transaction, and retain them in accordance with rule 30.1 to 30.3.

Application

10.5 This rule applies only to private practice. It does not cover money held or received by a donee of a power of attorney acting in a purely personal capacity outside any legal practice (see rule 4, guidance notes (iii)–(iv)).

10.6 A "*client's* own account" covers all accounts in a *client's* own name, whether opened by the *client* himself or herself, or by *you* on the *client's* instructions under rule 15.1(b). A "*client's* own account" also includes an account opened in the name of a person designated by the *client* under rule 15.1(b).

Guidance notes

(i) Money held in a client's own account (under a power of attorney or otherwise) is not "client money" for the purpose of the rules because it is not "held or received" by you. If you close the account and receive the closing balance, this becomes client money subject to all the rules.

(ii) Merely paying money into a client's own account, or helping the client to complete forms in relation to such an account, is not "operating" the account.

(iii) If as executor you operate the deceased's account (whether before or after the grant of probate), you will be subject to the limited requirements of rule 10. If the account is subsequently transferred into your name, or a new account is opened in your name, you will have "held or received" client money and are then subject to all the rules.

Rule 11: Firm's rights not affected

11.1 Nothing in these rules deprives *you* of any recourse or right, whether by way of lien, set off, counterclaim, charge or otherwise, against money standing to the credit of a *client account*.

Rule 12: Categories of money

12.1 These rules do not apply to *out-of-scope money*, save to the limited extent specified in the rules. All other money held or received in the course of practice falls into one or other of the following categories:

(a) "client money" – money held or received for a *client* or as *trustee*, and all other money which is not *office money*; or

(b) "office money" – money which belongs to *you* or *your firm*.

12.2 "Client money" includes money held or received:

(a) as *trustee*;

(b) as agent, bailee, stakeholder, or as the donee of a power of attorney, or as a liquidator, trustee in bankruptcy, *Court of Protection deputy* or trustee of an occupational pension scheme;

(c) for payment of unpaid *professional disbursements*;

(d) for payment of stamp duty land tax, Land Registry registration fees, telegraphic transfer fees and court fees (but see also guidance note (i));

(e) as a payment on account of *costs* generally;

(f) as a financial benefit paid in respect of a *client*, unless the *client* has given *you* prior authority to retain it (see Chapter 1, outcome 1.15 and indicative behaviour 1.20 of the *SRA Code of Conduct*);

(g) jointly with another person outside the *firm*.

12.3 Money held to the sender's order is *client money*.

(a) If money is accepted on such terms, it must be held in a *client account*.

(b) However, a cheque or draft sent to *you* on terms that the cheque or draft (as opposed to the money) is held to the sender's order must not be presented for payment without the sender's consent.

(c) The recipient is always subject to a professional obligation to return the money, or the cheque or draft, to the sender on demand.

12.4 An advance to a *client* which is paid into a *client account* under rule 14.2(b) becomes *client money*.

12.5 A cheque in respect of damages and *costs*, made payable to the *client* but paid into a *client account* under rule 14.2(e), becomes *client money*.

12.6 Endorsing a cheque or draft over to a *client* or employer in the course of practice amounts to receiving *client money*. Even if no other *client money* is held or received, *you* must comply with some provisions of the rules, e.g.:

(a) rule 7 (duty to remedy breaches);

(b) rule 29 (accounting records for client accounts, etc.);

(c) rule 31 (production of documents, information and explanations);

(d) rule 32A (obtaining and delivery of accountants' reports).

12.7 "Office money" includes:

(a) money held or received in connection with running the *firm*; for example, PAYE, or VAT on the *firm's fees*;

(b) *interest* on *general client accounts*; the *bank* or *building society* should be instructed to credit such *interest* to the *office account* – but see also rule 14.2(d);

(c) payments received in respect of:

 (i) *fees* due to the *firm* against a bill or written notification of *costs* incurred, which has been given or sent in accordance with rule 17.2;

 (ii) *disbursements* already paid by the *firm*;

 (iii) *disbursements* incurred but not yet paid by the *firm*, but excluding unpaid *professional disbursements*;

 (iv) money paid for or towards an *agreed fee*;

(d) money held in a *client account* and earmarked for *costs* under rule 17.3;

(e) money held or received from the Legal Aid Agency as a *regular payment* (see rule 19.2).

12.8 If a *firm* conducts a personal or office transaction – for instance, conveyancing – for a *principal* (or for a number of *principals*), money held or received on behalf of the *principal(s)* is *office money*. However, other circumstances may mean that the money is *client money*, for example:

(a) If the *firm* also acts for a lender, money held or received on behalf of the lender is *client money*.

(b) If the *firm* acts for a *principal* and, for example, his or her spouse jointly (assuming the spouse is not a *partner* in the practice), money received on their joint behalf is *client money*.

(c) If the *firm* acts for an assistant *solicitor*, consultant or non-solicitor employee, or (if it is a *company*) a *director*, or (if it is an *LLP*) a member, he or she is regarded as a *client* of the *firm*, and money received for him or her is *client money* – even if he or she conducts the matter personally.

Guidance notes

(i) Money held or received for payment of stamp duty land tax, Land Registry registration fees, telegraphic transfer fees and court fees is not office money because you have not incurred an obligation to HMRC, the Land Registry, the bank or the court to pay the duty or fee; (on the other hand, if you have already paid the duty or fee out of your own resources, or have received the service on credit, or the bank's charge for a telegraphic transfer forms part of your profit costs, payment subsequently received from the client will be office money);

(ii) Money held:

(a) by liquidators, trustees in bankruptcy, Court of Protection deputies and trustees of occupational pension schemes;

(b) jointly with another person outside the practice (for example, with a lay trustee, or with another firm);

is client money, subject to a limited application of the rules – see rules 8 and 9. The donee of a power of attorney, who operates the donor's own account, is also subject to a limited application of the rules (see rule 10), although money kept in the donor's own account is not "client money" because it is not "held or received" by the donee.

(iii) If the SRA intervenes in a practice, money from the practice is held or received by the SRA's intervention agent subject to a trust under Schedule 1 paragraph 7(1) of the Solicitors Act 1974, and is therefore client money. The same provision requires the agent to pay the money into a client account.

(iv) Money held or received in the course of employment when practising in one of the capacities listed in rule 5 (persons exempt from the rules) is not "client money" for the purpose of the rules, because the rules do not apply at all.

(v) The receipt of out-of-scope money of an MDP which is mixed with other types of money is dealt with in rules 17 and 18.

(vi) See Appendices 1 and 2 (which do not form part of the rules) for a summary of the effect of the rules and the treatment of different types of money.

PART 2: CLIENT MONEY AND OPERATION OF A CLIENT ACCOUNT

Rule 13: Client accounts

13.1 If *you* hold or receive *client money*, *you* must keep one or more *client accounts* (unless all the *client money* is always dealt with outside any *client account* in accordance with rule 8, rule 9, rule 15 or rule 16).

13.2 A "client account" is an account of a practice kept at a *bank* or *building society* for holding *client money*, in accordance with the requirements of this part of the rules.

13.3 The *client account(s)* of:

(a) a *sole practitioner* must be in the name under which the *sole practitioner* is recognised by the *SRA*, whether that is the *sole practitioner's* own name or the *firm* name;

(b) a *partnership* must be in the name under which the *partnership* is recognised by the *SRA*;

(c) an incorporated practice must be in the company name, or the name of the *LLP*, as registered at Companies House;

(d) in-house *solicitors* or *RELs* must be in the name of the current *principal solicitor/REL* or *solicitors/RELs*;

(e) *trustees*, where all the *trustees* of a *trust* are *managers* and/or employees of the same *recognised body* or *licensed body*, must be either in the name of the *recognised body/licensed body* or in the name of the *trustee(s)*;

(f) *trustees*, where all the *trustees* of a *trust* are the *sole practitioner* and/or his or her employees, must be either in the name under which the *sole practitioner* is recognised by the *SRA* or in the name of the *trustee(s)*;

and the name of the account must also include the word "client" in full (an abbreviation is not acceptable).

13.4 A *client account* must be:

(a) a *bank* account at a branch (or a *bank's* head office) in England and Wales; or

(b) a *building society* account at a branch (or a society's head office) in England and Wales.

13.5 There are two types of *client account*:

(a) a "separate designated client account", which is an account for money relating to a single *client*, other person or *trust*, and which includes in its title, in addition to the requirements of rule 13.3 above, a reference to the identity of the *client*, other person or *trust*; and

(b) a "general client account", which is any other *client account*.

13.6 [Deleted]

13.7 The *clients* of a *licensed body* must be informed at the outset of the retainer, or during the course of the retainer as appropriate, if the *licensed body* is (or becomes) owned by a *bank* or *building society* and its *client account* is held at that *bank* or *building society* (or another *bank* or *building society* in the same group).

13.8 Money held in a *client account* must be immediately available, even at the sacrifice of *interest*, unless the *client* otherwise instructs, or the circumstances clearly indicate otherwise.

Guidance notes

(i) In the case of in-house practice, any client account should include the names of all solicitors or registered European lawyers held out on the notepaper as principals. The names of other employees who are solicitors or registered European lawyers may also be included if so desired.

(ii) Compliance with rule 13.1 to 13.4 ensures that clients, as well as the bank or building society, have the protection afforded by section 85 of the Solicitors Act 1974 or article 4 of the Legal Services Act 2007 (Designation as a Licensing Authority) (No. 2) Order 2011 as appropriate.

Rule 14: Use of a client account

14.1 *Client money* must *without delay* be paid into a *client account*, and must be held in a *client account*, except when the rules provide to the contrary (see rules 8, 9, 15, 16, 17 and 19).

14.2 Only *client money* may be paid into or held in a *client account*, except:

(a) an amount of the *firm's* own money required to open or maintain the account;

(b) an advance from the *firm* to fund a payment on behalf of a *client* or *trust* in excess of funds held for that *client* or *trust*; the sum becomes *client money* on payment into the account (for *interest* on *client money*, see rule 22.2(c));

(c) money to replace any sum which for any reason has been drawn from the account in breach of rule 20; the replacement money becomes *client money* on payment into the account;

(d) *interest* which is paid into a *client account* to enable payment from the *client account* of all money owed to the *client*; and

(e) a cheque in respect of damages and *costs*, made payable to the *client*, which is paid into the *client account* pursuant to the *Society's* Conditional Fee Agreement; the sum becomes *client money* on payment into the account (but see rule 17.1(e) for the transfer of the *costs* element from *client account*);

and except when the rules provide to the contrary (see guidance note (ii) below).

14.3 *Client money* must be returned to the *client* (or other person on whose behalf the money is held) promptly, as soon as there is no longer any proper reason to retain those funds. Payments received after *you* have already accounted to the *client*, for example by way of a refund, must be paid to the *client* promptly.

14.4 *You* must promptly inform a *client* (or other person on whose behalf the money is held) in writing of the amount of any *client money* retained at the end of a matter (or the substantial conclusion of a matter), and the reason for that retention. *You* must inform the *client* (or other person) in writing at least once every twelve months thereafter of the amount of *client money* still held and the reason for the retention, for as long as *you* continue to hold that money.

14.5 *You* must not provide banking facilities through a *client account*. Payments into, and transfers or withdrawals from, a *client account* must be in respect of instructions relating to an underlying transaction (and the funds arising therefrom) or to a service forming part of *your* normal regulated activities.

Guidance notes

(i) Exceptions to rule 14.1 (client money must be paid into a client account) can be found in:

(a) rule 8 – liquidators, trustees in bankruptcy, Court of Protection deputies and trustees of occupational pension schemes;

(b) rule 9 – joint accounts;

(c) rule 15 – client's instructions;

(d) rule 16 – cash paid straight to client, beneficiary or third party;

(A) cheque endorsed to client, beneficiary or third party;

(B) money withheld from client account on the SRA's authority;

(C) money withheld from client account in accordance with a trustee's powers;

(e) rule 17.1(b) – receipt and transfer of costs;

(f) rule 19.1 – payments by the Legal Aid Agency.

(ii) Rule 14.2(a) to (e) provides for exceptions to the principle that only client money may be paid into a client account. Additional exceptions can be found in:

(a) rule 17.1(c) – receipt and transfer of costs;

(b) rule 18.2(b) – receipt of mixed payments;

(c) rule 19.2(c)(ii) – transfer to client account of a sum for unpaid professional disbursements, where regular payments are received from the Legal Aid Agency.

(iii) Only a nominal sum will be required to open or maintain an account. In practice, banks will usually open (and, if instructed, keep open) accounts with nil balances.

(iv) If client money is invested in the purchase of assets other than money – such as stocks or shares – it ceases to be client money, because it is no longer money held by the firm. If the investment is subsequently sold, the money received is, again, client money. The records kept under rule 29 will need to include entries to show the purchase or sale of investments.

(v) Rule 14.5 reflects decisions of the Solicitors Disciplinary Tribunal that it is not a proper part of a solicitor's everyday business or practice to operate a banking facility for third parties, whether they are clients of the firm or not. It should be noted that any exemption under the Financial Services and Markets Act 2000 is likely to be lost if a deposit is taken in circumstances which do not form part of your practice. It should also be borne in mind that there are criminal sanctions against assisting money launderers.

(vi) As with rule 7 (Duty to remedy breaches), "promptly" in rule 14.3 and 14.4 is not defined but should be given its natural meaning in the particular circumstances. Accounting to a client for any surplus funds will often fall naturally at the end of a matter. Other retainers may be more protracted and, even when the principal work has been completed, funds may still be needed, for example, to cover outstanding work in a conveyancing transaction or to meet a tax liability. (See also paragraphs 4.8 and 4.9 of the Guidelines for accounting procedures and systems at Appendix 3.)

(vii) There may be some instances when, during the course of a retainer, the specific purpose for which particular funds were paid no longer exists, for example, the need to instruct counsel or a medical expert. Rule 14.3 is concerned with returning funds to clients at the end of a matter (or the substantial conclusion of a matter) and is not intended to apply to ongoing retainers. However, in order to act in the best interests of your client, you may need to take instructions in such circumstances to ascertain, for instance, whether the money should be returned to the client or retained to cover the general funding or other aspects of the case.

(viii) See rule 20.1(j)–(k) for withdrawals from a client account when the rightful owner of funds cannot be traced. The obligation to report regularly under rule 14.4 ceases to apply if you are no longer able to trace the client, at which point rule 20.1(j) or (k) would apply.

Rule 15: Client money withheld from client account on client's instructions

15.1 *Client money* may be:

(a) held by *you* outside a *client account* by, for example, retaining it in the *firm's* safe in the form of cash, or placing it in an account in the *firm's* name which is not a *client account*, such as an account outside England and Wales; or

(b) paid into an account at a *bank*, *building society* or other financial institution opened in the name of the *client* or of a person designated by the *client*;

but only if the *client* instructs *you* to that effect for the *client's* own convenience, and only if the instructions are given in writing, or are given by other means and confirmed by *you* to the *client* in writing.

15.2 It is improper to seek blanket agreements, through standard terms of business or otherwise, to hold *client money* outside a *client account*.

15.3 If a *client* instructs *you* to hold part only of a payment in accordance with rule 15.1(a) or (b), the entire payment must first be placed in a *client account*, before transferring the relevant part out and dealing with it in accordance with the *client's* instructions.

15.4 A payment on account of *costs* received from a person who is funding all or part of *your fees* may be withheld from a *client account* on the instructions of that person given in accordance with rule 15.1.

Guidance notes

(i) Money withheld from a client account under rule 15.1(a) remains client money, and all the record-keeping provisions of rule 29 will apply.

(ii) Once money has been paid into an account set up under rule 15.1(b), it ceases to be client money. Until that time, the money is client money and, under rule 29, a record is required of your receipt of the money, and its payment into the account in the name of the client or designated person. If you can operate the account, rule 10 (operating a client's own account) and rule 30 (accounting records for clients' own accounts) will apply. In the absence of instructions to the contrary, rule 14.1 requires any money withdrawn to be paid into a client account.

(iii) Rule 29.17(d) requires clients' instructions under rule 15.1 to be kept for at least six years.

Rule 16: Other client money withheld from a client account

16.1 The following categories of *client money* may be withheld from a *client account*:

(a) cash received and *without delay* paid in cash in the ordinary course of business to the *client* or, on the *client's* behalf, to a third party, or paid in cash in the execution of a *trust* to a beneficiary or third party;

(b) a cheque or draft received and endorsed over in the ordinary course of business to the *client* or, on the *client's* behalf, to a third party, or *without delay* endorsed over in the execution of a *trust* to a beneficiary or third party;

(c) money withheld from a *client account* on instructions under rule 15;

(d) money which, in accordance with a *trustee's* powers, is paid into or retained in an account of the *trustee* which is not a *client account* (for example, an account outside England and Wales), or properly retained in cash in the performance of the *trustee's* duties;

(e) unpaid *professional disbursements* included in a payment of *costs* dealt with under rule 17.1(b);

(f) in respect of payments from the Legal Aid Agency:

(i) advance payments from the Legal Aid Agency withheld from *client account* (see rule 19.1(a)); and

(ii) unpaid *professional disbursements* included in a payment of *costs* from the Legal Aid Agency (see rule 19.1(b)); and

(g) money withheld from a *client account* on the written authorisation of the *SRA*. The *SRA* may impose a condition that the money is paid to a charity which gives an indemnity against any legitimate claim subsequently made for the sum received.

Guidance notes

(i) If money is withheld from a client account under rule 16.1(a) or (b), rule 29 requires records to be kept of the receipt of the money and the payment out.

(ii) If money is withheld from a client account under rule 16.1(d), rule 29 requires a record to be kept of the receipt of the money, and requires the inclusion of the money in the monthly reconciliations. (Money held by a trustee jointly with another party is subject only to the limited requirements of rule 9.)

(iii) It makes no difference, for the purpose of the rules, whether an endorsement is effected by signature in the normal way or by some other arrangement with the bank.

(iv) The circumstances in which authorisation would be given under rule 16.1(g) must be extremely rare. Applications for authorisation should be made to the Professional Ethics Guidance Team.

Rule 17: Receipt and transfer of costs

17.1 When *you* receive money paid in full or part settlement of *your* bill (or other notification of *costs*) *you* **must follow one of the following five options:**

- (a) **determine the composition of the payment without delay, and deal with the money accordingly:**
  - (i) if the sum comprises *office money* and/or *out-of-scope money* only, it must be placed in an *office account*;
  - (ii) if the sum comprises only *client money*, the entire sum must be placed in a *client account*;
  - (iii) if the sum includes both *office money* and *client money*, or *client money* and *out-of-scope money*, or *client money*, *out-of-scope money* and *office money*, *you* must follow rule 18 (receipt of mixed payments); or
- (b) **ascertain that the payment comprises only *office money* and/or *out-of-scope money*, and/or *client money* in the form of *professional disbursements* incurred but not yet paid, and deal with the payment as follows:**
  - (i) place the entire sum in an *office account* at a *bank* or *building society* branch (or head office) in England and Wales; and
  - (ii) by the end of the second working day following receipt, either pay any unpaid *professional disbursement*, or transfer a sum for its settlement to a *client account*; **or**
- (c) **pay the entire sum into a *client account* (regardless of its composition), and transfer any *office money* and/or *out-of-scope money* out of the *client account* within 14 days of receipt; or**
- (d) **on receipt of *costs* from the Legal Aid Agency, follow the option in rule 19.1(b); or**
- (e) **in relation to a cheque paid into a *client account* under rule 14.2(e), transfer the *costs* element out of the *client account* within 14 days of receipt.**

17.2 If *you* properly require payment of *your fees* from money held for a *client* or *trust* in a *client account*, *you* must first give or send a bill of *costs*, or other written notification of the *costs* incurred, to the *client* or the paying party.

17.3 Once *you* have complied with rule 17.2 above, the money earmarked for *costs* becomes *office money* and must be transferred out of the *client account* within 14 days.

17.4 A payment on account of *costs* generally in respect of those activities for which the practice is regulated by the *SRA* is *client money*, and must be held in a *client account* until *you* have complied with rule 17.2 above. (For an exception in the case of legal aid payments, see rule 19.1(a). See also rule 18 on dealing with mixed payments of *client money* and/or *out-of-scope money* when part of a payment on account of *costs* relates to activities not regulated by the *SRA*.)

17.5 A payment for an *agreed fee* must be paid into an *office account*. An "agreed fee" is one that is fixed – not a *fee* that can be varied upwards, nor a *fee* that is dependent on the transaction being completed. An *agreed fee* must be evidenced in writing.

17.6 *You* will not be in breach of rule 17 as a result of a misdirected electronic payment or other direct transfer from a *client* or paying third party, provided:

(a) appropriate systems are in place to ensure compliance;

(b) appropriate instructions were given to the *client* or paying third party;

(c) the *client's* or paying third party's mistake is remedied promptly upon discovery; and

(d) appropriate steps are taken to avoid future errors by the *client* or paying third party.

17.7 *Costs* transferred out of a *client account* in accordance with rule 17.2 and 17.3 must be specific sums relating to the bill or other written notification of *costs*, and covered by the amount held for the particular *client* or *trust*. Round sum withdrawals on account of *costs* are a breach of the rules.

17.8 In the case of a *trust* of which the only *trustee(s)* are within the *firm*, the paying party will be the *trustee(s)* themselves. *You* must keep the original bill or notification of *costs* on the file, in addition to complying with rule 29.15 (central record or file of copy bills, etc.).

17.9 Undrawn *costs* must not remain in a *client account* as a "cushion" against any future errors which could result in a shortage on that account, and cannot be regarded as available to set off against any general shortage on *client account*.

Guidance notes

(i) This note lists types of disbursement and how they are categorised:

(a) Money received for paid disbursements is office money.

(b) Money received for unpaid professional disbursements is client money.

(c) Money received for other unpaid disbursements for which you have incurred a liability to the payee (for example, travel agents' charges, taxi fares, courier charges or Land Registry search fees, payable on credit) is office money.

(d) Money received for disbursements anticipated but not yet incurred is a payment on account, and is therefore client money.

(ii) The option in rule 17.1(a) allows you to place all payments in the correct account in the first instance. The option in rule 17.1(b) allows the prompt banking into an office account of an invoice payment when the only uncertainty is whether or not the payment includes some client money in the form of unpaid professional disbursements. The option in rule 17.1(c) allows the prompt banking into a client account of any invoice payment in advance of determining whether the payment is a mixture of office and client money (of whatever description), or client money and out-of-scope money, or client money, out-of-scope money and office money, or is only office money and/or out-of-scope money.

(iii) If you are not in a position to comply with the requirements of rule 17.1(b), you cannot take advantage of that option.

(iv) The option in rule 17.1(b) cannot be used if the money received includes a payment on account – for example, a payment for a professional disbursement anticipated but not yet incurred.

(v) In order to be able to use the option in rule 17.1(b) for electronic payments or other direct transfers from clients, you may choose to establish a system whereby clients are given an office account number for payment of costs. The system must be capable of ensuring that, when invoices are sent to the client, no request is made for any client money, with the sole exception of money for professional disbursements already incurred but not yet paid.

(vi) Rule 17.1(c) allows clients to be given a single account number for making direct payments by electronic or other means – under this option, it has to be a client account.

(vii) "Properly" in rule 17.2 implies that the work has actually been done, whether at the end of the matter or at an interim stage, and that you are entitled to appropriate the money for costs. For example, the costs set out in a completion statement in a conveyancing transaction will become due on completion and should be transferred out of the client account within 14 days of completion in accordance with rule 17.3. The requirement to transfer costs out of the client account within a set time is intended to prevent costs being left on client account to conceal a shortage.

(viii) Money is "earmarked" for costs under rule 17.2 and 17.3 when you decide to use funds already held in client account to settle your bill. If you wish to obtain the client's prior approval, you will need to agree the amount to be taken with your client before issuing the bill to avoid the possibility of failing to meet the 14 day time limit for making the transfer out of client account. If you wish to retain the funds, for example, as money on account of costs on another matter, you will need to ask the client to send the full amount in settlement of the bill. If, when submitting a bill, you fail to indicate whether you intend to take your costs from client account, or expect the client to make a payment, you will be regarded as having "earmarked" your costs.

(ix) An amendment to section 69 of the Solicitors Act 1974 by the Legal Services Act 2007 permits a solicitor or recognised body to sue on a bill which has been signed electronically and which the client has agreed can be delivered electronically.

(x) The rules do not require a bill of costs for an agreed fee, although your VAT position may mean that in practice a bill is needed. If there is no bill, the written evidence of the agreement must be filed as a written notification of costs under rule 29.15(b).

(xi) The bill of an MDP may be in respect of costs for work of the SRA-regulated part of the practice, and also for work that falls outside the scope of SRA regulation. Money received in respect of the non-SRA regulated work, including money for disbursements, is out-of-scope money and must be dealt with in accordance with rule 17.

(xii) See Chapter 1, indicative behaviour 1.21 of the SRA Code of Conduct in relation to ensuring that disbursements included in a bill reflect the actual amount spent or to be spent.

Rule 18: Receipt of mixed payments

18.1 A "mixed payment" is one which includes *client money* as well as *office money* and/or *out-of-scope money*.

18.2 A *mixed payment* must either:

(a) be split between a *client account* and *office account* as appropriate; or

(b) be placed *without delay* in a *client account*.

18.3 If the entire payment is placed in a *client account*, all *office money* and/or *out-of-scope money* must be transferred out of the *client account* within 14 days of receipt.

Guidance notes

(i) See rule 17.1(b) and (c) for additional ways of dealing with (among other things) mixed payments received in response to a bill or other notification of costs.

(ii) See rule 19.1(b) for (among other things) mixed payments received from the Legal Aid Agency.

(iii) Some out-of-scope money may be subject to the rules of other regulators which may require an earlier withdrawal from the client account operated under these rules.

Rule 19: Treatment of payments to legal aid practitioners

Payments from the Legal Aid Agency

19.1 Two special dispensations apply to payments (other than *regular payments*) from the Legal Aid Agency:

(a) An advance payment, which may include *client money*, may be placed in an *office account*, provided the Legal Aid Agency instructs in writing that this may be done.

(b) A payment for *costs* (interim and/or final) may be paid into an *office account* at a *bank* or *building society* branch (or head office) in England and Wales, regardless of whether it consists wholly of *office money*, or is mixed with *client money* in the form of:

(i) advance payments for *fees* or *disbursements*; or

(ii) money for unpaid *professional disbursements*;

provided all money for payment of *disbursements* is transferred to a *client account* (or the *disbursements* paid) within 14 days of receipt.

19.2 The following provisions apply to *regular payments* from the Legal Aid Agency:

(a) "Regular payments" (which are *office money*) are:

(i) standard monthly payments paid by the Legal Aid Agency under the civil legal aid contracting arrangements;

(ii) standard monthly payments paid by the Legal Aid Agency under the criminal legal aid contracting arrangements; and

(iii) any other payments for work done or to be done received from the Legal Aid Agency under an arrangement for payments on a regular basis.

(b) *Regular payments* must be paid into an *office account* at a *bank* or *building society* branch (or head office) in England and Wales.

(c) *You* must within 28 days of submitting a report to the Legal Aid Agency, notifying completion of a matter, either:

(i) pay any unpaid *professional disbursement(s)*, or

(ii) transfer to a *client account* a sum equivalent to the amount of any unpaid *professional disbursement(s)*, relating to that matter.

(d) In cases where the Legal Aid Agency permits *you* to submit reports at various stages during a matter rather than only at the end of a matter, the requirement in rule 19.2(c) above applies to any unpaid *professional disbursement(s)* included in each report so submitted.

Payments from a third party

19.3 If the Legal Aid Agency has paid any *costs* to *you* or a previously nominated *firm* in a matter (advice and assistance or legal help *costs*, advance payments or interim *costs*), or has paid *professional disbursements* direct, and *costs* are subsequently settled by a third party:

(a) The entire third party payment must be paid into a *client account*.

(b) A sum representing the payments made by the Legal Aid Agency must be retained in the *client account*.

(c) Any balance belonging to *you* must be transferred to an *office account* within 14 days of *your* sending a report to the Legal Aid Agency containing details of the third party payment.

(d) The sum retained in the *client account* as representing payments made by the Legal Aid Agency must be:

(i) **either** recorded in the individual *client's* ledger account, and identified as the Legal Aid Agency's money;

(ii) **or** recorded in a ledger account in the Legal Aid Agency's name, and identified by reference to the *client* or matter;

and kept in the *client account* until notification from the Legal Aid Agency that it has recouped an equivalent sum from subsequent payments due to *you*. The retained sum must be transferred to an *office account* within 14 days of notification.

19.4 Any part of a third party payment relating to unpaid *professional disbursements* or outstanding *costs* of the *client's* previous *firm* is *client money*, and must be kept in a *client account* until *you* pay the *professional disbursement* or outstanding *costs*.

Guidance notes

(i) This rule deals with matters which specifically affect legal aid practitioners. It should not be read in isolation from the remainder of the rules which apply to everyone, including legal aid practitioners.

(ii) In cases carried out under public funding certificates, firms can apply for advance payments ("Payments on Account" under the Standard Civil Contract). The Legal Aid Agency has agreed that these payments may be placed in office account.

(iii) Rule 19.1(b) deals with the specific problems of legal aid practitioners by allowing a mixed or indeterminate payment of costs (or even a payment consisting entirely of unpaid professional disbursements) to be paid into an office account, which for the purpose of rule 19.1(b) must be an account at a bank or building society. However, it is always open to you to comply with rule 17.1(a) to (c), which are the options for everyone for the receipt of costs. For regular payments, see guidance notes (v)–(vii) below.

(iv) Firms are required by the Legal Aid Agency to report promptly to the Legal Aid Agency on receipt of costs from a third party. It is advisable to keep a copy of the report on the file as proof of compliance with the Legal Aid Agency's requirements, as well as to demonstrate compliance with the rule.

(v) Rule 19.2(c) permits a firm, which is required to transfer an amount to cover unpaid professional disbursements into a client account, to make the transfer from its own resources if the regular payments are insufficient.

(vi) The 28 day time limit for paying, or transferring an amount to a client account for, unpaid professional disbursements is for the purposes of these rules only. An earlier deadline may be imposed by contract with the Legal Aid Agency or with counsel, agents or experts. On the other hand, you may have agreed to pay later than 28 days from the submission of the report notifying completion of a matter, in which case rule 19.2(c) will require a transfer of the appropriate amount to a client account (but not payment) within 28 days.

(vii) For the appropriate accounting records for regular payments, see rule 29.7.

Rule 20: Withdrawals from a client account

20.1 *Client money* may only be withdrawn from a *client account* when it is:

(a) properly required for a payment to or on behalf of the *client* (or other person on whose behalf the money is being held);

(b) properly required for a payment in the execution of a particular *trust*, including the purchase of an investment (other than money) in accordance with the *trustee's* powers;

(c) properly required for payment of a *disbursement* on behalf of the *client* or *trust*;

(d) properly required in full or partial reimbursement of money spent by *you* on behalf of the *client* or *trust*;

(e) transferred to another *client account*;

(f) withdrawn on the *client's* instructions, provided the instructions are for the *client's* convenience and are given in writing, or are given by other means and confirmed by *you* to the *client* in writing;

(g) transferred to an account other than a *client account* (such as an account outside England and Wales), or retained in cash, by a *trustee* in the proper performance of his or her duties;

(h) a refund to *you* of an advance no longer required to fund a payment on behalf of a *client* or *trust* (see rule 14.2(b));

(i) money which has been paid into the account in breach of the rules (for example, money paid into the wrong *separate designated client account*) – see rule 20.5 below;

(j) money not covered by (a) to (i) above, where *you* comply with the conditions set out in rule 20.2; or

(k) money not covered by (a) to (i) above, withdrawn from the account on the written authorisation of the *SRA*. The *SRA* may impose a condition that *you* pay the money to a charity which gives an indemnity against any legitimate claim subsequently made for the sum received.

20.2 A withdrawal of *client money* under rule 20.1(j) above may be made only where the amount held does not exceed £500 in relation to any one individual *client* or *trust* matter and *you*:

(a) establish the identity of the owner of the money, or make reasonable attempts to do so;

(b) make adequate attempts to ascertain the proper destination of the money, and to return it to the rightful owner, unless the reasonable costs of doing so are likely to be excessive in relation to the amount held;

(c) pay the funds to a charity;

(d) record the steps taken in accordance with rule 20.2(a)–(c) above and retain those records, together with all relevant documentation (including receipts from the charity), in accordance with rule 29.16 and 29.17(a); and

(e) keep a central register in accordance with rule 29.22.

20.3 *Office money* may only be withdrawn from a *client account* when it is:

(a) money properly paid into the account to open or maintain it under rule 14.2(a);

(b) properly required for payment of *your costs* under rule 17.2 and 17.3;

(c) the whole or part of a payment into a *client account* under rule 17.1(c);

(d) part of a *mixed payment* placed in a *client account* under rule 18.2(b); or

(e) money which has been paid into a *client account* in breach of the rules (for example, *interest* wrongly credited to a *general client account*) – see rule 20.5 below.

20.4 *Out-of-scope money* must be withdrawn from a *client account* in accordance with rules 17.1(a), 17.1(c) and 18 as appropriate.

20.5 Money which has been paid into a *client account* in breach of the rules must be withdrawn from the *client account* promptly upon discovery.

20.6 Money withdrawn in relation to a particular *client* or *trust* from a *general client account* must not exceed the money held on behalf of that *client* or *trust* in all *your general client accounts* (except as provided in rule 20.7 below).

20.7 *You* may make a payment in respect of a particular *client* or *trust* out of a *general client account*, even if no money (or insufficient money) is held for that *client* or *trust* in *your general client account(s)*, provided:

(a) sufficient money is held for that *client* or *trust* in a *separate designated client account*; and

(b) the appropriate transfer from the *separate designated client account* to a *general client account* is made immediately.

20.8 Money held for a *client* or *trust* in a *separate designated client account* must not be used for payments for another *client* or *trust*.

20.9 A *client account* must not be overdrawn, except in the following circumstances:

(a) A *separate designated client account* operated in *your* capacity as *trustee* can be overdrawn if *you* make payments on behalf of the *trust* (for example, inheritance tax) before realising sufficient assets to cover the payments.

(b) If a *sole practitioner* dies and his or her *client accounts* are frozen, overdrawn *client accounts* can be operated in accordance with the rules to the extent of the money held in the frozen accounts.

Guidance notes

(i) Withdrawals in favour of firm, and for payment of disbursements

(a) Disbursements to be paid direct from a client account, or already paid out of your own money, can be withdrawn under rule 20.1(c) or (d) in advance of preparing a bill of costs. Money to be withdrawn from a client account for the payment of costs (fees and disbursements) under rule 17.2 and 17.3 becomes office money and is dealt with under rule 20.3(b).

(b) Money is "spent" under rule 20.1(d) at the time when you despatch a cheque, unless the cheque is to be held to your order. Money is also regarded as "spent" by the use of a credit account, so that, for example, search fees, taxi fares and courier charges incurred in this way may be transferred to your office account.

(c) See rule 21.4 for the way in which a withdrawal from a client account in your favour must be effected.

(ii) Cheques payable to banks, building societies, etc.

(a) In order to protect client money against misappropriation when cheques are made payable to banks, building societies or other large institutions, it is strongly recommended that you add the name and number of the account after the payee's name.

(iii) Drawing against uncleared cheques

(a) You should use discretion in drawing against a cheque received from or on behalf of a client before it has been cleared. If the cheque is not met, other clients' money will have been used to make the payment in breach of the rules (see rule 7 (duty to remedy breaches)). You may be able to avoid a breach of the rules by instructing the bank or building society to charge all unpaid credits to your office or personal account.

(iv) Non-receipt of electronic payments

(a) If you withdraw money from a general client account on the strength of information that an electronic payment is on its way, but the electronic payment does not arrive, you will have used other clients' money in breach of the rules. See also rule 7 (duty to remedy breaches).

(v) Withdrawals on instructions

(a) One of the reasons why a client might authorise a withdrawal under rule 20.1(f) might be to have the money transferred to a type of account other than a client account. If so, the requirements of rule 15 must be complied with.

(vi) Withdrawals where the rightful owner cannot be traced, on the SRA's authorisation and without SRA authorisation

(a) Applications for authorisation under rule 20.1(k) should be made to the Professional Ethics Guidance Team, who can advise on the criteria which must normally be met for authorisation to be given. You may under rule 20.1(j) pay to a charity sums of £500 or less per client or trust matter without the SRA's authorisation, provided the safeguards set out in rule 20.2 are followed.

(b) You will need to apply to the SRA, whatever the amount involved, if the money to be withdrawn is not to be paid to a charity. This situation might arise, for example, if you have been unable to deliver a bill of costs because the client has become untraceable and so cannot make a transfer from client account to office account in accordance with rule 17.2–17.3.

(c) After a practice has been wound up, surplus balances are sometimes discovered in an old client account. This money remains subject to rule 20 and rule 21. An application can be made to the SRA under rule 20.1(k).

Rule 21: Method of and authority for withdrawals from client account

21.1 A withdrawal from a *client account* may be made only after a specific authority in respect of that withdrawal has been signed by an appropriate person or persons in accordance with the *firm's* procedures for signing on *client account*. An authority for withdrawals from *client account* may be signed electronically, subject to appropriate safeguards and controls.

21.2 *Firms* must put in place appropriate systems and procedures governing withdrawals from *client account*, including who should be permitted by the *firm* to sign on *client account*. A non-*manager* owner or a non-employee owner of a *licensed body* is not an appropriate person to be a signatory on *client account* and must not be permitted by the *firm* to act in this way.

21.3 There is no need to comply with rule 21.1 above when transferring money from one *general client account* to another *general client account* at the same *bank* or *building society*.

21.4 A withdrawal from a *client account* in *your* favour must be either by way of a cheque, or by way of a transfer to the *office account* or to *your* personal account. The withdrawal must not be made in cash.

Guidance notes

(i) A firm should select suitable people to authorise withdrawals from the client account. Firms will wish to consider whether any employee should be able to sign on client account, and whether signing rights should be given to all managers of the practice or limited to those managers directly involved in providing legal services. Someone who has no day-to-day involvement in the business of the practice is unlikely to be regarded as a suitable signatory because of the lack of proximity to client matters. An appropriate understanding of the requirements of the rules is essential – see paragraph 4.2 of the Guidelines for accounting procedures and systems at Appendix 3.

(ii) Instructions to the bank or building society to withdraw money from a client account (rule 21.1) may be given over the telephone, provided a specific authority has been signed in accordance with this rule before the instructions are given. It is of paramount importance that there are appropriate in-built safeguards, such as passwords, to give the greatest protection possible for client money. Suitable safeguards will also be needed for practices which operate a CHAPS terminal or other form of electronic instruction for payment.

(iii) In the case of a withdrawal by cheque, the specific authority (rule 21.1) is usually a signature on the cheque itself. Signing a blank cheque is not a specific authority.

(iv) A withdrawal from a client account by way of a private loan from one client to another can only be made if the provisions of rule 27.2 are complied with.

(v) If, in your capacity as trustee, you instruct an outside administrator to run, or continue to run, on a day-to-day basis, the business or property portfolio of an estate or trust, you will not need to comply with rule 21.1, provided all cheques are retained in accordance with rule 29.18. (See also rule 29, guidance note (ii)(d).)

(vi) You may set up a "direct debit" system of payment for Land Registry application fees on either the office account or a client account. If a direct debit payment is to be taken from a client account for the payment of Land Registry application fees, a signature, which complies with the firm's systems and procedures set up under rule 21, on the application for registration will constitute the specific authority required by rule 21.1. As with any other payment method, care must be taken to ensure that sufficient uncommitted funds are held in the client account for the particular client before signing the authority. You should also bear in mind that should the Land Registry take an incorrect amount in error from a firm's client account (for example, a duplicate payment), the firm will be in breach of the rules if other clients' money has been used as a result.

(vii) If you fail to specify the correct Land Registry fee on the application for registration (either by specifying a lesser amount than that actually due, or failing to specify any fee at all), you will be in breach of rule 21.1 if the Land Registry takes a sum from your client account greater than that specified on the application, without a specific authority for the revised sum being in place as required by rule 21. In order that you can comply with the rules, the Land Registry will need to contact you before taking the revised amount, so that the necessary authority may be signed prior to the revised amount being taken.

(viii) Where the Land Registry contacts you by telephone, and you wish to authorise an immediate payment by direct debit over the telephone, you will first need to check that there is sufficient money held in client account for the client and, if there is, that it is not committed to some other purpose.

(ix) The specific authority required by rule 21.1 can be signed after the telephone call has ended but must be signed before the additional payment (or correct full payment) is taken by the Land Registry. It is advisable to sign the authority promptly and, in any event, on the same day as the telephone instruction is given to the Land Registry to take the additional (or correct full) amount. If you decide to fund any extra amount from the office account, the transfer of office money to the client account would need to be made, preferably on the same day but, in any event, before the direct debit is taken. Your internal procedures would need to make it clear how to deal with such situations; for example, who should be consulted before a direct debit for an amount other than that specified on the application can be authorised, and the mechanism for ensuring the new authority is signed by a person permitted by the firm to sign on client account.

(x) You may decide to set up a direct debit system of payment on the office account because, for example, you do not wish to allow the Land Registry to have access to the firm's client account. Provided you are in funds, a transfer from the client account to the office account may be made under rule 20.1(d) to reimburse you as soon as the direct debit has been taken.

(xi) Variable "direct debit" payments to the Land Registry, as described in guidance notes (vi)–(x) above, are not direct debits in the usual sense as each payment is authorised and confirmed individually. A traditional direct debit or standing order should not be set up on a client account because of the need for a specific authority for each withdrawal.

PART 3: INTEREST

Rule 22: When interest must be paid

22.1 When *you* hold money in a *client account* for a *client*, or for a person funding all or part of *your fees*, or for a *trust*, *you* must account to the *client* or that person or *trust* for *interest* when it is fair and reasonable to do so in all the circumstances. (This also applies if money should have been held in a *client account* but was not. It also applies to money held in an account in accordance with rule 15.1(a) (or which should have been held in such an account), or rule 16.1(d).)

22.2 *You* are not required to pay *interest*:

(a) on money held for the payment of a *professional disbursement*, once counsel etc. has requested a delay in settlement;

(b) on money held for the Legal Aid Agency;

(c) on an advance from *you* under rule 14.2(b) to fund a payment on behalf of the *client* or *trust* in excess of funds held for that *client* or *trust*; or

(d) if there is an agreement to contract out of the provisions of this rule under rule 25.

22.3 *You* must have a written policy on the payment of *interest*, which seeks to provide a fair outcome. The terms of the policy must be drawn to the attention of the *client* at the outset of a retainer, unless it is inappropriate to do so in the circumstances.

Guidance notes

(i) Requirement to pay interest

(a) Money is normally held for a client as a necessary, but incidental, part of the retainer, to facilitate the carrying out of the client's instructions. The main purpose of the rules is to keep that money safe and available for the purpose for which it was provided. The rules also seek to provide for the payment of a fair sum of interest, when appropriate, which is unlikely to be as high as that obtainable by the client depositing those funds.

(b) An outcomes-focused approach has been adopted in this area, allowing firms the flexibility to set their own interest policies in order to achieve a fair outcome for both the client and the firm.

(c) In addition to your obligation under rule 22.3, it is good practice to explain your interest arrangements to clients. These will usually be based on client money being held in an instant access account to facilitate a transaction.

Clients are unlikely to receive as much interest as might have been obtained had they held and invested the money themselves. A failure to explain the firm's policy on interest may lead to unrealistic expectations and, possibly, a complaint to the Legal Ombudsman.

(d) The Legal Services Act 2007 has abolished the distinction in the Solicitors Act 1974 between interest earned on client money held in a general client account or a separate designated client account, meaning that interest earned on the latter type of account is, in theory, to be accounted for like interest on any other client money on a "fair and reasonable" basis. In practice, however, a firm which wishes to retain any part of the interest earned on client money will need to hold that money in a general client account and continue to have interest paid to the office account (see rule 12.7(b)). The tax regime still treats interest arising on money held in a separate designated client account as belonging to the client, and requires banks to deduct tax at source from that interest (subject to the tax status of the individual client) and credit the interest to the separate designated client account. This makes it impracticable for firms to retain any part of the interest earned on a separate designated client account.

(e) Some firms may wish to apply a de minimis by reference to the amount held and period for which it was held, for example, providing that no interest is payable if the amount calculated on the balance held is £20 or less. Any de minimis will need to be set at a reasonable level and regularly reviewed in the light of current interest rates.

(f) It is likely to be appropriate for firms to account for all interest earned in some circumstances, for example, where substantial sums of money are held for lengthy periods of time.

(g) If sums of money are held in relation to separate matters for the same client, it is normally appropriate to treat the money relating to the different matters separately but there may be cases when the matters are so closely related that they ought to be considered together, for example, when you are acting for a client in connection with numerous debt collection matters. Similarly, it may be fair and reasonable in the circumstances to aggregate sums of money held intermittently during the course of acting for a client.

(h) There is no requirement to pay interest on money held on instructions under rule 15.1(a) in a manner which attracts no interest.

(i) Accounts opened in the client's name under rule 15.1(b) (whether operated by you or not) are not subject to rule 22, as the money is not held by you. All interest earned belongs to the client. The same applies to any account in the client's own name operated by you as signatory under rule 10.

(ii) Interest policy (rule 22.3)

(a) It is important that your clients should be aware of the terms of your interest policy. This should normally be covered at the outset of a retainer, although it may be unnecessary where you have acted for the client previously. It is open to you and your client to agree that interest will be dealt with in a different way (see rule 25).

(iii) Unpresented cheques

(a) A client may fail to present a cheque to his or her bank for payment. Whether or not it is reasonable to recalculate the amount due will depend on all the circumstances of the case. A reasonable charge may be made for any extra work carried out if you are legally entitled to make such a charge.

(iv) Liquidators, trustees in bankruptcy, Court of Protection deputies and trustees of occupational pension schemes

(a) Under rule 8, Part 3 of the rules does not normally apply to liquidators, etc. You must comply with the appropriate statutory rules and regulations, and rule 8.3 and 8.4 as appropriate.

(v) Joint accounts

(a) Under rule 9, Part 3 of the rules does not apply to joint accounts. If you hold money jointly with a client, interest earned on the account will be for the benefit of the client unless otherwise agreed. If money is held jointly with another practice, the allocation of interest earned will depend on the agreement reached.

(vi) Failure to pay interest

(a) A client, including one of joint clients, or a person funding all or part of your fees, may complain to the Legal Ombudsman if he or she believes that interest was due and has not been paid, or that the amount paid was insufficient. It is advisable for the client (or other person) to try to resolve the matter with you before approaching the Legal Ombudsman.

Rule 23: Amount of interest

23.1 The *interest* paid must be a fair and reasonable sum calculated over the whole period for which the money is held.

Guidance notes

(i) You will usually account to the client for interest at the conclusion of the client's matter, but might in some cases consider it appropriate to account to the client at intervals throughout.

(ii) The sum paid by way of interest need not necessarily reflect the highest rate of interest obtainable but it is unlikely to be appropriate to look only at the lowest rate of interest obtainable. A firm's policy on the calculation of interest will need to take into account factors such as:

(a) the amount held;

(b) the length of time for which cleared funds were held;

(c) the need for instant access to the funds;

(d) the rate of interest payable on the amount held in an instant access account at the bank or building society where the client account is kept;

(e) the practice of the bank or building society where the client account is kept in relation to how often interest is compounded.

(iii) A firm needs to have regard to the effect of the overall banking arrangements negotiated between it and the bank, on interest rates payable on individual balances. A fair sum of interest is unlikely to be achieved by applying interest rates which are set at an artificially low level to reflect, for example, more favourable terms in relation to the firm's office account.

(iv) A firm might decide to apply a fixed rate of interest by reference, for example, to the base rate. In setting that rate, the firm would need to consider (and regularly review) the level of interest it actually receives on its client accounts, but also take into account its overall banking arrangements so far as they affect the rates received.

(v) When looking at the period over which interest must be calculated, it will usually be unnecessary to check on actual clearance dates. When money is received by cheque and paid out by cheque, the normal clearance periods will usually cancel each other out, so that it will be satisfactory to look at the period between the dates when the incoming cheque is banked and the outgoing cheque is drawn.

(vi) Different considerations apply when payments in and out are not both made by cheque. So, for example, the relevant periods would normally be:

(a) from the date when you receive incoming money in cash until the date when the outgoing cheque is sent;

(b) from the date when an incoming telegraphic transfer begins to earn interest until the date when the outgoing cheque is sent;

(c) from the date when an incoming cheque or banker's draft is or would normally be cleared until the date when the outgoing telegraphic transfer is made or banker's draft is obtained.

(vii) Rule 13.8 requires that money held in a client account must be immediately available, even at the sacrifice of interest, unless the client otherwise instructs, or the circumstances clearly indicate otherwise. The need for access can be taken into account in assessing the appropriate rate for calculating interest to be paid.

(viii) For failure to pay a sufficient sum by way of interest, see guidance note (vi)(a) to rule 22.

Rule 24: Interest on stakeholder money

24.1 When *you* hold money as stakeholder, *you* must pay *interest* on the basis set out in rule 22 to the person to whom the stake is paid, unless the parties have contracted out of this provision (see rule 25.3).

Rule 25: Contracting out

25.1 In appropriate circumstances *you* and *your client* may by a written agreement come to a different arrangement as to the matters dealt with in rule 22 (payment of interest).

25.2 *You* must act fairly towards *your clients* when entering into an agreement to depart from the *interest* provisions, including providing sufficient information at the outset to enable them to give informed consent.

25.3 When acting as stakeholder *you* may, by a written agreement with *your* own *client* and the other party to the transaction, come to a different arrangement as to the matters dealt with in rule 22.

Guidance notes

(i) Whether it is appropriate to contract out depends on all the circumstances, for example, the size of the sum involved or the nature, status or bargaining position of the client. It might, for instance, be appropriate to contract out by standard terms of business if the client is a substantial commercial entity and the interest involved is modest in relation to the size of the transaction. The larger the sum of interest involved, the more there would be an onus on you to show that a client who had accepted a contracting out provision was properly informed and had been treated fairly.

(ii) Contracting out which on the face of it appears to be against the client's interests is permissible where the client has given informed consent. For example, some clients may wish to contract out for reasons related to their tax position or to comply with their religious beliefs.

(iii) A firm which decides not to receive or pay interest, due to the religious beliefs of its principals, will need to ensure that clients are informed at the outset, so that they can choose to instruct another firm if the lack of interest is an issue for them.

(iv) Another example of contracting out is when the client stipulates, and the firm agrees, that all interest earned should be paid to the client despite the terms of the firm's interest policy.

(v) In principle, you are entitled to make a reasonable charge to the client for acting as stakeholder in the client's matter.

(vi) Alternatively, it may be appropriate to include a special provision in the contract that you retain the interest on the deposit to cover your charges for acting as stakeholder. This is only acceptable if it will provide a fair and reasonable payment for the work and risk involved in holding a stake. The contract could stipulate a maximum charge, with any interest earned above that figure being paid to the recipient of the stake.

(vii) Any right to charge the client, or to stipulate for a charge which may fall on the client, would be excluded by, for instance, a prior agreement with the client for a fixed fee for the client's matter, or for an estimated fee which cannot be varied upwards in the absence of special circumstances. It is therefore not normal practice for a stakeholder in conveyancing transactions to receive a separate payment for holding the stake.

(viii) A stakeholder who seeks an agreement to exclude the operation of rule 24 should be particularly careful not to take unfair advantage either of the client, or of the other party if unrepresented.

PART 4: ACCOUNTING SYSTEMS AND RECORDS

Rule 26: Guidelines for accounting procedures and systems

26.1 The *SRA* may from time to time publish guidelines for accounting procedures and systems to assist *you* to comply with Parts 1 to 4 of the rules, and *you* may be required to justify any departure from the guidelines.

Guidance notes

(i) The current guidelines appear at Appendix 3.

Rule 27: Restrictions on transfers between clients

27.1 A paper transfer of money held in a *general client account* from the ledger of one *client* to the ledger of another *client* may only be made if:

(a) it would have been permissible to withdraw that sum from the account under rule 20.1; and

(b) it would have been permissible to pay that sum into the account under rule 14;

(but there is no requirement in the case of a paper transfer for a written authority under rule 21.1).

27.2 No sum in respect of a *private loan* from one *client* to another can be paid out of funds held for the lender either:

(a) by a payment from one *client account* to another;

(b) by a paper transfer from the ledger of the lender to that of the borrower; or

(c) to the borrower directly,

except with the prior written authority of both *clients*.

27.3 If a *private loan* is to be made by (or to) joint *clients*, the consent of each *client* must be obtained.

Rule 28: Executor, trustee or nominee companies

28.1 If *your firm* owns all the shares in a *recognised body* or a *licensed body* which is an executor, trustee or nominee company, *your firm* and the *recognised body* or *licensed body* must not operate shared *client accounts*, but may:

(a) use one set of accounting records for money held, received or paid by the *firm* and the *recognised body* or *licensed body*; and/or

(b) deliver a single accountant's report for both the *firm* and the *recognised body* or *licensed body*.

28.2 If such a *recognised body* or *licensed body* as nominee receives a dividend cheque made out to the *recognised body* or *licensed body*, and forwards the cheque, either endorsed or subject to equivalent instructions, to the share-owner's *bank* or *building society*, etc., the *recognised body* or *licensed body* will have received (and paid) *client money*. One way of complying with rule 29 (accounting records) is to keep a copy of the letter to the share-owner's *bank* or *building society*, etc., on the file, and, in accordance with rule 29.23, to keep another copy in a central book of such letters. (See also rule 29.17(f) (retention of records for six years)).

Rule 29: Accounting records for client accounts, etc.

Accounting records which must be kept

29.1 *You* must at all times keep accounting records properly written up to show *your* dealings with:

(a) *client money* received, held or paid by *you*; including *client money* held outside a *client account* under rule 15.1(a) or rule 16.1(d); and

(b) any *office money* relating to any *client* or *trust* matter.

29.2 All dealings with *client money* must be appropriately recorded:

(a) in a client cash account or in a record of sums transferred from one client ledger account to another; and

(b) on the client side of a separate client ledger account for each *client* (or other person, or *trust*).

No other entries may be made in these records.

29.3 If *separate designated client accounts* are used:

(a) a combined cash account must be kept in order to show the total amount held in *separate designated client accounts*; and

(b) a record of the amount held for each *client* (or other person, or *trust*) must be made either in a deposit column of a client ledger account, or on the client side of a client ledger account kept specifically for a *separate designated client account*, for each *client* (or other person, or *trust*).

29.4 All dealings with *office money* relating to any *client* matter, or to any *trust* matter, must be appropriately recorded in an office cash account and on the office side of the appropriate client ledger account.

29.5 A cheque or draft received on behalf of a *client* and endorsed over, not passing through a *client account*, must be recorded in the books of account as a receipt and payment on behalf of the *client*. The same applies to cash received and not deposited in a *client account* but paid out to or on behalf of a *client*.

29.6 Money which has been paid into a *client account* under rule 17.1(c) (receipt of costs), or rule 18.2(b) (mixed money), and for the time being remains in a *client account*, is to be treated as *client money*; it must be appropriately identified and recorded on the client side of the client ledger account.

29.7 Money which has been paid into an *office account* under rule 17.1(b) (receipt of costs), rule 19.1(a) (advance payments from the Legal Aid Agency), or rule 19.1(b) (payment of costs from the Legal Aid Agency), and for the time being remains in an *office account* without breaching the rules, is to be treated as *office money*. Money paid into an *office account* under rule 19.2(b) (regular payments) is *office money*. All these payments must be appropriately identified and recorded on the office side of the client ledger account for the individual *client* or for the Legal Aid Agency.

29.8 *Client money* in a currency other than sterling must be held in a separate account for the appropriate currency, and *you* must keep separate books of account for that currency.

Current balance

29.9 The current balance on each client ledger account must always be shown, or be readily ascertainable, from the records kept in accordance with rule 29.2 and 29.3 above.

Acting for both lender and borrower

29.10 When acting for both lender and borrower on a mortgage advance, separate client ledger accounts for both *clients* need not be opened, provided that:

(a) the funds belonging to each *client* are clearly identifiable; and

(b) the lender is an institutional lender which provides mortgages on standard terms in the normal course of its activities.

Statements from banks, building societies and other financial institutions

29.11 *You* must, at least every 5 weeks:

(a) obtain hard copy statements (or duplicate statements permitted in lieu of the originals by rule 9.3 or 9.4 from *banks*, *building societies* or other financial institutions, or

(b) obtain and save in the *firm's* accounting records, in a format which cannot be altered, an electronic version of the *bank's*, *building society's* or other financial institution's on-line record,

in respect of:

(i) any *general client account* or *separate designated client account*;

(ii) any joint account held under rule 9;

(iii) any account which is not a *client account* but in which *you* hold *client money* under rule 15.1(a) or rule 16.1(d); and

(iv) any *office account* maintained in relation to the *firm*;

and each statement or electronic version must begin at the end of the previous statement.

This provision does not apply in respect of passbook-operated accounts, nor in respect of the *office accounts* of an *MDP* operated solely for activities not subject to *SRA* regulation.

Reconciliations

29.12 *You* must, at least once every five weeks:

(a) compare the balance on the client cash account(s) with the balances shown on the statements and passbooks (after allowing for all unpresented items) of all *general client accounts* and *separate designated client accounts*, and of any account which is not a *client account* but in which *you* hold *client money* under rule 15.1(a) or rule 16.1(d), and any *client money* held by *you* in cash; and

(b) as at the same date prepare a listing of all the balances shown by the client ledger accounts of the liabilities to *clients* (and other persons, and *trusts*) and compare the total of those balances with the balance on the client cash account; and also

(c) prepare a reconciliation statement; this statement must show the cause of the difference, if any, shown by each of the above comparisons.

29.13 Reconciliations must be carried out as they fall due, or at the latest by the due date for the next reconciliation. In the case of a *separate designated client account* operated with a passbook, there is no need to ask the *bank*, *building society* or other financial institution for confirmation of the balance held. In the case of other *separate designated client accounts*, *you* must either obtain statements at least monthly or written confirmation of the balance direct from the *bank*, *building society* or other financial institution. There is no requirement to check that *interest* has been credited since the last statement, or the last entry in the passbook.

29.14 All shortages must be shown. In making the comparisons under rule 29.12(a) and (b), *you* must not, therefore, use credits of one *client* against debits of another when checking total client liabilities.

Bills and notifications of costs

29.15 *You* must keep readily accessible a central record or file of copies of:

(a) all bills given or sent by *you* (other than those relating entirely to activities not regulated by the *SRA*); and

(b) all other written notifications of *costs* given or sent by *you* (other than those relating entirely to activities not regulated by the *SRA*).

Withdrawals under rule 20.1(j)

29.16 If *you* withdraw *client money* under rule 20.1(j) *you* must keep a record of the steps taken in accordance with rule 20.2(a)–(c), together with all relevant documentation (including receipts from the charity).

Retention of records

29.17 *You* must retain for at least six years from the date of the last entry:

(a) all documents or other records required by rule 29.1 to 29.10, 29.12, and 29.15 to 29.16 above;

(b) all statements required by rule 29.11(a) above and passbooks, as printed and issued by the *bank*, *building society* or other financial institution; and/or all on-line records obtained and saved in electronic form under rule 29.11(b) above, for:

(i) any *general client account* or *separate designated client account*;

(ii) any joint account held under rule 9;

(iii) any account which is not a *client account* but in which *you* hold *client money* under rule 15.1(a) or rule 16.1(d); and

(iv) any *office account* maintained in relation to the practice, but not the *office accounts* of an *MDP* operated solely for activities not subject to *SRA* regulation;

(c) any records kept under rule 8 (liquidators, trustees in bankruptcy, Court of Protection deputies and trustees of occupational pension schemes) including, as printed or otherwise issued, any statements, passbooks and other accounting records originating outside *your* office;

(d) any written instructions to withhold *client money* from a *client account* (or a copy of *your* confirmation of oral instructions) in accordance with rule 15;

(e) any central registers kept under rule 29.19 to 29.22 below; and

(f) any copy letters kept centrally under rule 28.2 (dividend cheques endorsed over by nominee company).

29.18 *You* must retain for at least two years:

(a) originals or copies of all authorities, other than cheques, for the withdrawal of money from a *client account*; and

(b) all original paid cheques (or digital images of the front and back of all original paid cheques), unless there is a written arrangement with the *bank*, *building society* or other financial institution that:

(i) it will retain the original cheques on *your* behalf for that period; or

(ii) in the event of destruction of any original cheques, it will retain digital images of the front and back of those cheques on *your* behalf for that period and will, on demand by *you*, *your* reporting accountant or the *SRA*, produce copies of the digital images accompanied, when requested, by a certificate of verification signed by an authorised officer.

(c) The requirement to keep paid cheques under rule 29.18(b) above extends to all cheques drawn on a *client account*, or on an account in which *client money* is held outside a *client account* under rule 15.1(a) or rule 16.1(d).

(d) Microfilmed copies of paid cheques are not acceptable for the purposes of rule 29.18(b) above. If a *bank*, *building society* or other financial institution is able to provide microfilmed copies only, *you* must obtain the original paid cheques from the *bank* etc. and retain them for at least two years.

Centrally kept records for certain accounts, etc.

29.19 Statements and passbooks for *client money* held outside a *client account* under rule 15.1(a) or rule 16.1(d) must be kept together centrally, or *you* must maintain a central register of these accounts.

29.20 Any records kept under rule 8 (liquidators, trustees in bankruptcy, Court of Protection deputies and trustees of occupational pension schemes) must be kept together centrally, or *you* must maintain a central register of the appointments.

29.21 The statements, passbooks, duplicate statements and copies of passbook entries relating to any joint account held under rule 9 must be kept together centrally, or *you* must maintain a central register of all joint accounts.

29.22 A central register of all withdrawals made under rule 20.1(j) must be kept, detailing the name of the *client*, other person or *trust* on whose behalf the money is held (if known), the amount, the name of the recipient charity and the date of the payment.

29.23 If a nominee company follows the option in rule 28.2 (keeping instruction letters for dividend payments), a central book must be kept of all instruction letters to the share-owner's *bank* or *building society*, etc.

Computerisation

29.24 Records required by this rule may be kept on a computerised system, apart from the following documents, which must be retained as printed or otherwise issued:

(a) original statements and passbooks retained under rule 29.17(b) above;

(b) original statements, passbooks and other accounting records retained under rule 29.17(c) above; and

(c) original cheques and original hard copy authorities retained under rule 29.18 above.

There is no obligation to keep a hard copy of computerised records. However, if no hard copy is kept, the information recorded must be capable of being reproduced reasonably quickly in printed form for at least six years, or for at least two years in the case of digital images of paid cheques retained under rule 29.18 above.

Suspense ledger accounts

29.25 Suspense client ledger accounts may be used only when *you* can justify their use; for instance, for temporary use on receipt of an unidentified payment, if time is needed to establish the nature of the payment or the identity of the *client*.

Guidance notes

(i) It is strongly recommended that accounting records are written up at least weekly, even in the smallest practice, and daily in the case of larger firms.

(ii) Rule 29.1 to 29.10 (general record-keeping requirements) and rule 29.12 (reconciliations) do not apply to:

(a) liquidators, trustees in bankruptcy, Court of Protection deputies and trustees of occupational pension schemes operating in accordance with statutory rules or regulations under rule 8.1(i);

(b) joint accounts operated under rule 9;

(c) a client's own account operated under rule 10; the record-keeping requirements for this type of account are set out in rule 30;

(d) you in your capacity as a trustee when you instruct an outside administrator to run, or continue to run, on a day-to-day basis, the business or property portfolio of an estate or trust, provided the administrator keeps and retains appropriate accounting records, which are available for inspection by the SRA in accordance with rule 31. (See also guidance note (v) to rule 21.)

(iii) A cheque made payable to a client, which is forwarded to the client by you, is not client money and falls outside the rules, although it is advisable to record the action taken. See rule 14.2(e) for the treatment of a damages cheque, made payable to the client, which you pay into a client account under the Law Society's Conditional Fee Agreement.

(iv) Some accounting systems do not retain a record of past daily balances. This does not put you in breach of rule 29.9.

(v) "Clearly identifiable" in rule 29.10 means that by looking at the ledger account the nature and owner of the mortgage advance are unambiguously stated. For example, if a mortgage advance of £100,000 is received from the ABC Building Society, the entry should be recorded as "£100,000, mortgage advance, ABC Building Society". It is not enough to state that the money was received from the ABC Building Society without specifying the nature of the payment, or vice versa.

(vi) Although you do not open a separate ledger account for the lender, the mortgage advance credited to that account belongs to the lender, not to the borrower, until completion takes place. Improper removal of these mortgage funds from a client account would be a breach of rule 20.

(vii) Section 67 of the Solicitors Act 1974 permits a solicitor or recognised body to include on a bill of costs any disbursements which have been properly incurred but not paid before delivery of the bill, subject to those disbursements being described on the bill as unpaid.

(viii) Rule 29.17(d) – retention of client's instructions to withhold money from a client account – does not require records to be kept centrally; however this may be prudent, to avoid losing the instructions if the file is passed to the client.

(ix) You may enter into an arrangement whereby the bank keeps digital images of paid cheques in place of the originals. The bank should take an electronic image of the front and back of each cheque in black and white and agree to hold such images, and to make printed copies available on request, for at least two years. Alternatively, you may take and keep your own digital images of paid cheques.

(x) Certificates of verification in relation to digital images of cheques may on occasion be required by the SRA when exercising its investigative and enforcement powers. The reporting accountant will not need to ask for a certificate of verification but will be able to rely on the printed copy of the digital image as if it were the original.

(xi) These rules require an MDP to keep accounting records only in respect of those activities for which it is regulated by the SRA. Where an MDP acts for a client in a matter which includes activities regulated by the SRA, and activities outside the SRA's regulatory reach, the accounting records should record the MDP's dealings in respect of the SRA-regulated part of the client's matter. It may also be necessary to include in those records dealings with out-of-scope money where that money has been handled in connection with, or relates to, the SRA-regulated part of the transaction. An MDP is not required to maintain records in respect of client matters which relate entirely to activities not regulated by the SRA.

Rule 30: Accounting records for clients' own accounts

30.1 When *you* operate a *client's* own account as signatory under rule 10, *you* must retain, for at least six years from the date of the last entry, the statements or passbooks as printed and issued by the *bank*, *building society* or other financial institution, and/or the duplicate statements, copies of passbook entries and cheque details permitted in lieu of the originals by rule 10.3 or 10.4; and any central register kept under rule 30.2 below.

30.2 *You* must either keep these records together centrally, or maintain a central register of the accounts operated under rule 10.

30.3 If *you* use on-line records made available by the *bank*, *building society* or other financial institution, *you* must save an electronic version in the *firm's* accounting records in a format which cannot be altered. There is no obligation to keep a hard copy but the information recorded must be capable of being reproduced reasonably quickly in printed form for at least six years.

30.4 If, when *you* cease to operate the account, the *client* requests the original statements or passbooks, *you* must take photocopies and keep them in lieu of the originals.

30.5 This rule applies only to private practice.

PART 5: MONITORING AND INVESTIGATION BY THE SRA

Rule 31: Production of documents, information and explanations

31.1 *You* must at the time and place fixed by the *SRA* produce to any person appointed by the *SRA* any records, papers, *client* and *trust* matter files, financial accounts and other documents, and any other information, necessary to enable preparation of a report on compliance with the rules.

31.2 A requirement for production under rule 31.1 above must be in writing, and left at or sent by post or document exchange to the most recent address held by the *SRA's* Information Directorate, or sent electronically to the *firm's* e-mail or fax address, or delivered by the *SRA's* appointee. A notice under this rule is deemed to be duly served:

(a) on the date on which it is delivered to or left at *your* address;

(b) on the date on which it is sent electronically to *your* e-mail or fax address; or

(c) 48 hours (excluding Saturdays, Sundays and Bank Holidays) after it has been sent by post or document exchange.

31.3 Material kept electronically must be produced in the form required by the *SRA's* appointee.

31.4 The *SRA's* appointee is entitled to seek verification from *clients* and staff, and from the *banks*, *building societies* and other financial institutions used by *you*. *You* must, if necessary, provide written permission for the information to be given.

31.5 The *SRA's* appointee is not entitled to take original documents away but must be provided with photocopies on request.

31.6 *You* must be prepared to explain and justify any departures from the Guidelines for accounting procedures and systems published by the *SRA* (see rule 26).

31.7 Any report made by the *SRA's* appointee may, if appropriate, be sent to the Crown Prosecution Service or the Serious Fraud Office and/or used in proceedings before the Solicitors Disciplinary Tribunal. In the case of an *REL* or *RFL*, the report may also be sent to the competent authority in that lawyer's home state or states. In the case of a *solicitor* who is established in another state under the *Establishment Directive*, the report may also be sent to the competent authority in the host state. The report may also be sent to any of the accountancy bodies set out in rule 34.1(a) and/or taken into account by the *SRA* in relation to a possible disqualification of a reporting accountant under rule 34.3.

31.8 Without prejudice to rule 31.1 above, *you* must produce documents relating to any account kept by *you* at a *bank* or with a *building society*:

(a) in connection with *your* practice; or

(b) in connection with any *trust* of which *you* are or formerly were a *trustee*,

for inspection by a person appointed by the *SRA* for the purpose of preparing a report on compliance with the rules or on whether the account has been used for or in connection with a breach of any of the Principles or other SRA Handbook requirements made or issued by the *SRA*. Rules 31.2–31.7 above apply in relation to this paragraph in the same way as to rule 31.1.

Guidance notes

(i) The SRA's powers override any confidence or privilege between you and the client.

(ii) The SRA's monitoring and investigation powers are exercised by Forensic Investigations.

(iii) The SRA will normally give a brief statement of the reasons for its investigations and inspections but not if the SRA considers that there is a risk that disclosure could:

(a) breach any duty of confidentiality;

(b) disclose, or risk disclosure of, a confidential source of information;

(c) significantly increase the risk that those under investigation may destroy evidence, seek to influence witnesses, default, or abscond; or

(d) otherwise prejudice or frustrate an investigation or other regulatory action.

PART 6: ACCOUNTANTS' REPORTS

Rule 32: Delivery of accountants' reports

[Deleted]

Rule 32A: Obtaining and delivery of accountants' reports

32A.1 Subject to rule 32A.1A, if *you* have, at any time during an *accounting period*, held or received *client money*, or operated a *client's* own account as signatory, *you* must:

(a) obtain an accountant's report for that *accounting period* within six months of the end of the *accounting period*; and

(b) if the report has been qualified, deliver it to the SRA within six months of the end of the *accounting period*.

This duty extends to the *directors* of a *company*, or the members of an *LLP*, which is subject to this rule.

32A.1A Subject to rule 32A.2, *you* are not required to obtain or deliver an accountant's report if:

(a) all of the *client money* held or received during an *accounting period* is money held or received from the Legal Aid Agency or in the circumstances set out in rule 19.3; or

(b) in the *accounting period*, the statement or passbook balance of client money you have held or received does not exceed:

(i) an average of £10,000; and

(ii) a maximum of £250,000,

or the equivalent in foreign currency.

32A.1B In rule 32A.1A above:

(a) a "statement or passbook balance" is the total balance obtained at least once every five weeks, from a bank, building society or other institution of all *general client accounts* and *separate designated client accounts*, and accounts that are not *client accounts* but are holding *client money*, when carrying out reconciliations in accordance with rules 29.11 to 29.14; and

(b) an average "statement or passbook balance" is the total of all statement or passbook balances obtained in any *accounting period* divided by the number of such balances in that period.

32A.2 Notwithstanding the provisions of rules 32A.1 and 32A.1A, the SRA may require *you* to obtain or deliver an accountant's report at any time in circumstances other than those set out in rules 32A.1 and in the circumstances set out in rule 32A.1A if the SRA has reason to believe that it is in the public interest to do so.

Guidance notes

(i) A qualified accountant's report is a report prepared in accordance with rule 32A.1(a) where the reporting accountant forms the judgement that these rules have not been complied with such that the safety of client money is at risk. The form of the report is dealt with in rule 44. See also the SRA's "Guidance to Reporting Accountants and firms on planning and completion of the annual Accountants' Reports, under Rule 32A of the SRA Accounts Rules 2011".

(ii) To qualify for the exemption in rule 32A.1A(b), you are required to assess at the end of the accounting period if the average (at least five weekly) balance of client money you have held or received is or less than, or equal to £10,000 and that the maximum aggregated total of client money held or received is less than, or equal to £250,000 (or the equivalent in foreign currency). Both thresholds need to be satisfied for the exemption to apply. If you do satisfy the criteria you will be exempted from the requirement of obtaining an annual accountant's report for that accounting period. We expect that firms will inevitably move in and out of the thresholds from year to year and it is your obligation to satisfy yourself, and if required the SRA, that you have properly applied the exemptions. You should ensure you keep full records of your decisions in this regard. For the avoidance of any doubt if you or your firm is exempted from the obligation to obtain an accountant's report under rule 32A.1A, all of the other sections of these rules will continue to apply to you in full.

(iii) Examples of situations under rule 32A.2 include:

- (a) when no report has been obtained or delivered but the SRA has reason to believe that a report should have been obtained or delivered, for example, because you have failed to deliver a qualified report to the SRA or where you have failed to obtain a report because you have improperly applied one of the exemptions in rule 32A.1A;
- (b) when a report has been delivered but the SRA has reason to believe that it may be inaccurate;
- (c) when your conduct gives the SRA reason to believe that it would be appropriate to require you to obtain or deliver a report earlier than would otherwise have been the case (for instance three months after the end of the accounting period);
- (d) when your conduct gives the SRA reason to believe that it would be appropriate to require the obtaining and delivery of a report, whether or not qualified that an exemption would otherwise apply, or the more frequent obtaining and delivery of reports (for instance every six months);
- (e) when the SRA has reason to believe that the regulatory risk justifies the imposition on a category of firm of a requirement to obtain and deliver reports earlier or at more frequent intervals;

(f) when a condition on a solicitor's practising certificate requires earlier delivery of reports or the obtaining and delivery of reports at more frequent intervals.

(iv) The requirement in rule 32A for a registered foreign lawyer to deliver an accountant's report applies only to a registered foreign lawyer practising in one of the ways set out in paragraph (vi)(C) of the definition of "you" in the Glossary.

(v) When client money is held or received by an unincorporated practice, the principals in the practice will have held or received client money. A salaried partner whose name appears in the list of partners on a firm's letterhead, even if the name appears under a separate heading of "salaried partners" or "associate partners", is a principal.

(vi) In the case of an incorporated practice, it is the company or LLP (i.e. the recognised body or licensed body) which will have held or received client money. The recognised body/licensed body and its directors (in the case of a company) or members (in the case of an LLP) will have the duty to obtain the accountant's report and to deliver any such report to the SRA if it is qualified, although the directors or members will not usually have held client money.

(vii) Assistant solicitors, consultants and other employees do not normally hold client money. An assistant solicitor or consultant might be a signatory for a firm's client account, but this does not constitute holding or receiving client money. If a client or third party hands cash to an assistant solicitor, consultant or other employee, it is the sole principal or the partners (rather than the assistant solicitor, consultant or other employee) who are regarded as having received and held the money. In the case of an incorporated practice, whether a company or an LLP, it would be the recognised body or licensed body itself which would be regarded as having held or received the money.

(viii) If, exceptionally, an assistant solicitor, consultant or other employee has a client account (as a trustee), or operates a client's own account as signatory, the assistant solicitor, consultant or other employee will have to obtain and deliver an accountant's report unless the exemptions in rule 32A.1A apply. The assistant solicitor, consultant or other employee can be included in the report of the practice, but will need to ensure that his or her name is added, and an explanation given.

(ix) Rule 32A does not apply to a solicitor or registered European lawyer, employed as an in-house lawyer by a non-solicitor employer, who operates the account of the employer or a related body of the employer.

(x) In exceptional circumstances, a waiver of the obligation to obtain a report may sometimes be granted. Applications should be made to the SRA.

(xi) If a firm owns all the shares in a recognised body or licensed body which is an executor, trustee or nominee company, the firm and the recognised body/licensed body may obtain a single accountant's report (see rule 28.1(b)).

Rule 33: Accounting periods

The norm

33.1 An "accounting period" means the period for which *your* accounts are ordinarily made up, except that it must:

(a) begin at the end of the previous *accounting period*; and

(b) cover twelve months.

Rules 33.2 to 33.5 below set out exceptions.

First and resumed reports

33.2 If *you* are under a duty to obtain *your* first report, the *accounting period* must begin:

(a) on the date when *you* first held or received *client money* (or operated a *client's* own account as signatory); or

(b) at the end of the last *accounting period* in which an exemption under rule 32A.1A applied.

33.3 If *you* are under a duty to obtain *your* first report after a break, the *accounting period* must begin:

(a) on the date when *you*, for the first time after the break, held or received *client money* (or operated a *client's* own account as signatory); or

(b) at the end of the last *accounting period* in which an exemption under rule 32A.1A applied

and may cover less than twelve months.

Change of accounting period

33.4 If *you* change the period for which *your* accounts are made up (for example, on a merger, or simply for convenience), the *accounting period* immediately preceding the change may be shorter than twelve months, or longer than twelve months up to a maximum of 18 months, provided that the *accounting period* shall not be changed to a period longer than twelve months unless the *SRA* receives written notice of the change before expiry of the deadline for delivery of the accountant's report which would have been expected on the basis of *your* old *accounting period*.

Final reports

33.5 If *you* for any reason stop holding or receiving *client money* (and operating any *client's* own account as signatory), *you* must obtain and deliver a final report to the *SRA*. The *accounting period* must end on the date upon which *you* stopped holding or receiving *client money* (and operating any *client's* own account as signatory), and may cover less than twelve months.

Guidance notes

(i) You must obtain and deliver a final report to the SRA when you cease to hold client money. This applies regardless of whether you would otherwise have been exempted from the requirement to obtain an annual accountant's report on the basis you meet the criteria set out in Rule 32A.1A above and irrespective of whether the report is qualified or unqualified.

(ii) For a person who did not previously hold or receive client money, etc., and has become a principal in the firm, the report for the firm will represent, from the date of joining, that person's first report for the purpose of rule 33.2. For a person who was a principal in the firm and, on leaving, stops holding or receiving client money, etc., the report for the firm will represent, up to the date of leaving, that person's final report for the purpose of rule 33.5 above.

(iii) When a partnership splits up, it is usually appropriate for the books to be made up as at the date of dissolution, and for an accountant's report to be delivered within six months of that date. If, however, the old partnership continues to hold or receive client money, etc., in connection with outstanding matters, accountant's reports will continue to be required for those matters; the books should then be made up on completion of the last of those matters and a report delivered within six months of that date. The same would be true for a sole practitioner winding up matters on retirement.

(iv) When a practice is being wound up, you may be left with money which is unattributable, or belongs to a client who cannot be traced. It may be appropriate to apply to the SRA for authority to withdraw this money from the client account – see rule 20.1(k) and guidance note (vi)(a) to rule 20.

Rule 34: Qualifications for making a report

34.1 A report must be prepared and signed by an accountant:

(a) **who is a member of:**

(i) the Institute of Chartered Accountants in England and Wales;

(ii) the Institute of Chartered Accountants of Scotland;

(iii) the Association of Chartered Certified Accountants;

(iv) the Institute of Chartered Accountants in Ireland; or

(v) the Association of Authorised Public Accountants; **and**

(b) **who is also:**

(i) an individual who is a registered auditor within the terms of section 1239 of the Companies Act 2006; or

(ii) an employee of such an individual; or

(iii) a *partner* in or employee of a *partnership* which is a registered auditor within the terms of section 1239 of the Companies Act 2006; or

(iv) a director or employee of a company which is a registered auditor within the terms of section 1239 of the Companies Act 2006; or

(v) a member or employee of an *LLP* which is a registered auditor within the terms of section 1239 of the Companies Act 2006.

34.2 An accountant is not qualified to make a report if:

(a) at any time between the beginning of the *accounting period* to which the report relates, and the completion of the report:

(i) he or she was a *partner* or employee, or an officer or employee (in the case of a company), or a member or employee (in the case of an *LLP*) in the *firm* to which the report relates; or

(ii) he or she was employed by the same *non-solicitor employer* as the *solicitor* or *REL* for whom the report is being made; or

(iii) he or she was a *partner* or employee, or an officer or employee (in the case of a company), or a member or employee (in the case of an *LLP*) in an accountancy practice which had an ownership interest in, or was part of the group structure of, the *licensed body* to which the report relates; or

(b) he or she has been disqualified under rule 34.3 below and notice of disqualification has been given under rule 34.4 (and has not subsequently been withdrawn).

34.3 The *SRA* may disqualify an accountant from making any accountant's report if:

(a) the accountant has been found guilty by his or her professional body of professional misconduct or discreditable conduct; or

(b) the *SRA* is satisfied that *you* have not complied with the rules in respect of matters which the accountant has negligently failed to specify in a report.

In coming to a decision, the *SRA* will take into account any representations made by the accountant or his or her professional body.

34.4 Written notice of disqualification must be left at or sent by recorded delivery to the address of the accountant shown on an accountant's report or in the records of the accountant's professional body. If sent through the post, receipt will be deemed 48 hours (excluding Saturdays, Sundays and Bank Holidays) after posting.

34.5 An accountant's disqualification may be notified to any *firm* likely to be affected and may be printed in the *Society's* Gazette or other publication.

Guidance note

(i) It is not a breach of the rules for you to retain an outside accountant to write up the books of account and to instruct the same accountant to prepare the accountant's report. However, both you and the accountant will have to be satisfied that these circumstances do not affect his or her independence in preparing the report.

Rule 35: Reporting accountant's rights and duties – letter of engagement

35.1 *You* must ensure that the reporting accountant's rights and duties are stated in a letter of engagement incorporating the following terms:

"In accordance with rule 35 of the SRA Accounts Rules 2011, you are instructed as follows:

(a) I/this firm/this company/this limited liability partnership recognises that, if during the course of preparing an accountant's report:

(i) you discover evidence of fraud or theft in relation to money

(A) held by a solicitor (or registered European lawyer, or registered foreign lawyer, or recognised body, or licensed body, or employee of a solicitor or registered European lawyer, or manager or employee of a recognised body or licensed body) for a client or any other person (including money held on trust), or

(B) held in an account of a client, or an account of another person, which is operated by a solicitor (or registered European lawyer, registered foreign lawyer, recognised body, licensed body, employee of a solicitor or registered European lawyer, or manager or employee of a recognised body or licensed body); or

(ii) you obtain information which you have reasonable cause to believe is likely to be of material significance in determining whether a solicitor (or registered European lawyer, or registered foreign lawyer, or recognised body, or licensed body, or employee of a solicitor or registered European lawyer, or manager or employee of a recognised body or licensed body) is a fit and proper person

(A) to hold money for clients or other persons (including money held on trust), or

(B) to operate an account of a client or an account of another person,

(iii) you discover a failure by the firm to submit a qualified accountant's report to the Solicitors Regulation Authority, as required by these rules,

you must immediately give a report of the matter to the Solicitors Regulation Authority in accordance with section 34(9) of the Solicitors Act 1974 or article 3(1) of the Legal Services Act 2007 (Designation as a Licensing Authority) (No. 2) Order 2011 as appropriate;

(b) you may, and are encouraged to, make that report without prior reference to me/this firm/this company/this limited liability partnership;

(c) you are to report directly to the Solicitors Regulation Authority should your appointment be terminated following the issue of, or indication of intention to issue, a qualified accountant's report, or following the raising of concerns prior to the preparation of an accountant's report;

(d) you are to deliver to me/this firm/this company/this limited liability partnership your report which you should also retain for at least six years from the date of its signature and to produce the copy to the Solicitors Regulation Authority on request;

(e) you are to retain these terms of engagement for at least six years after the termination of the retainer and to produce them to the Solicitors Regulation Authority on request; and

(f) following any direct report made to the Solicitors Regulation Authority under (a) or (c) above, you are to provide to the Solicitors Regulation Authority on request any further relevant information in your possession or in the possession of your firm.

To the extent necessary to enable you to comply with (a) to (f) above, I/we waive my/the firm's/the company's/the limited liability partnership's right of confidentiality. This waiver extends to any report made, document produced or information disclosed to the Solicitors Regulation Authority in good faith pursuant to these instructions, even though it may subsequently transpire that you were mistaken in your belief that there was cause for concern."

35.2 The letter of engagement and a copy must be signed by *you* and by the accountant. *You* must keep the copy of the signed letter of engagement for at least six years after the termination of the retainer and produce it to the *SRA* on request. Both *you* and the reporting accountant must also retain a copy of the accountant's report, whether qualified or not, for at least six years from the date of its signature and produce the copy to the *SRA* on request.

35.3 The specified terms may be included in a letter from the accountant to *you* setting out the terms of the engagement but the text must be adapted appropriately. The letter must be signed in duplicate by both parties, with *you* keeping the original and the accountant the copy.

Guidance note

(i) Any direct report by the accountant to the SRA under rule 35.1(a) or (c) should be made to the Fraud and Confidential Intelligence Bureau.

Rule 36: Change of accountant

36.1 On instructing an accountancy practice to replace that previously instructed to produce accountant's reports, *you* must immediately notify the *SRA* of the change and provide the name and business address of the new accountancy practice.

Rule 37: Place of examination

[Deleted]

Rule 38: Provision of details of bank accounts, etc.

38.1 The accountant must request, and *you* must provide, details of all accounts kept or operated by *you* in connection with *your* practice at any *bank*, *building society* or other financial institution at any time during the *accounting period* to which the report relates. This includes *client accounts*, *office accounts*, accounts which are not *client accounts* but which contain *client money*, and *clients'* own accounts operated by *you* as signatory.

Rule 39: Test procedures

[Deleted]

Rule 40: Departures from guidelines for accounting procedures and systems

[Deleted]

Rule 41: Matters outside the accountant's remit

[Deleted]

Rule 42: Privileged documents

[Deleted]

Rule 43: Completion of checklist

[Deleted]

Rule 43A: Work to be undertaken

43A.1 The accountant should exercise his or her professional judgement in determining the work required for the firm they are instructed to obtain the report on in order to assess risks to *client money* arising from compliance with these rules. This should cover the work that the accountant considers is appropriate to enable completion of the report required by the *SRA* at the date the report is commissioned (referred to in Rule 44 below).

Guidance notes

(i) The purpose of the accountant's report is to enable a proportionate degree of oversight by the SRA over risks to clients' funds. It may also help the firm identify any improvements in its control systems that are required. The form of the report that the accountant is required to complete is intended to provide assurance that client funds are properly safeguarded. If the accountant forms the judgement that these Rules have not been complied with such that the safety of client money is at risk, then the accountant is required to "qualify" the report and set out in the report details of the areas where risks have been identified. Rule 32A.1 sets out which firms are required to obtain a report but only qualified reports have to be delivered to the SRA within the time frame set out.

(ii) The types of work that the accountant is required to undertake will depend on a number of factors including the size and complexity of the firm, the nature of the work undertaken, the number of transactions and amount of client funds held. The accountant may also want to consider the firm's existing systems and for example, the numbers and types of breaches of these Rules that the firm's COFA has recorded under his/her reporting obligations. Separate guidance as to the work that might be considered as part of a work programme has been issued by the SRA and will be updated from time to time; see the SRA's "Guidance to Reporting Accountants and firms on planning and completion of the annual Accountants' Reports, under Rule 32A of the SRA Accounts Rules 2011".

Rule 43B: Failure to provide documentation

43B.1 *You* must provide documentation to the accountant as required to enable completion of the accountant's report. When acting on a *client's* instructions, *you* will normally have the right on the grounds of privilege as between *solicitor* and *client* to decline to produce any document requested by the accountant for the purposes of his or her examination. A significant failure to provide documentation may result in the accountant deciding that they should qualify the report if they consider that as a result, they cannot properly prepare the report in accordance with these rules.

Guidance note

(i) In a recognised body or licensed body with one or more managers who are not legally qualified, legal professional privilege may not attach to work which is neither done nor supervised by a legally qualified individual – see Legal Services Act 2007, section 190(3) to (7), and Schedule 22, paragraph 17.

Rule 44: Form of accountant's report

44.1 The accountant must complete and sign his or her report in the form published from time to time by the *SRA*.

Guidance notes

(i) The current form of the accountant's report under rule 44 requires the accountant to confirm of he/she has found it necessary to qualify the report. If so, the report must be delivered to the SRA – see rule 32A.1(b) and guidance notes to that rule.

(ii) Separate reports can be obtained for each principal in a partnership but most firms choose to obtain one report in the name of all the principals. In either case, the report must be delivered to the SRA if it is qualified – see rule 32A.1(b) and the guidance notes to that rule. For assistant solicitors, consultants and other employees, see rule 32A, guidance notes (vii) and (viii).

(iii) An incorporated practice will obtain only one report, on behalf of the company and its directors, or on behalf of the LLP and its members – see rule 32A.1. The report must be delivered to the SRA if it is qualified – see rule 32A.1(b) and the guidance notes to that rule.

(iv) Although it may be agreed that the accountant will send a qualified report direct to the SRA, the responsibility for delivery is that of the firm. The form of report requires the accountant to confirm that a copy of the report (whether qualified or unqualified) has been sent to the COFA on behalf of the firm to which it relates. The COFA should ensure that the report is seen by each of the managers of the firm.

(v) For direct reporting by the accountant to the SRA in cases of concern, see rule 35 and guidance note (i) to that rule.

Rule 45: Firms with two or more places of business

45.1 If a *firm* has two or more offices:

- (a) separate reports may be obtained in respect of the different offices; and
- (b) separate *accounting periods* may be adopted for different offices, provided that:
  - (i) separate reports are obtained;
  - (ii) every office is covered by a report obtained within six months of the end of its *accounting period*; and
  - (iii) there are no gaps between the *accounting periods* covered by successive reports for any particular office or offices.

Rule 46: Waivers

46.1 The *SRA* may waive in writing in any particular case or cases any of the provisions of Part 6 of the rules, and may revoke any waiver.

Guidance note

(i) Applications for waivers should be made to the SRA. In appropriate cases, firms may be granted a waiver of the obligation to obtain an accountant's and in accordance with the SRA's current Waivers Policy.

PART 7: PRACTICE AS AN REL FROM AN OFFICE IN ENGLAND AND WALES OF AN EXEMPT EUROPEAN PRACTICE

Rule 47: Purpose of the overseas accounts provisions

[Deleted]

Rule 47A: Purpose of rules applying to RELs in Exempt European Practices

47A.1 The purpose of applying different accounts provisions to the practice of an *REL* from an office in England and Wales of an *Exempt European Practice* is to ensure similar protection for *client monies* but by way of rules which recognise that the body in which the *REL* is practising is not itself a regulated entity.

Rule 48: Application and Interpretation

48.1 Part 7 of these rules applies to your practice as an *REL* from an office in England and Wales of an *Exempt European Practice.*

48.2 The SRA Handbook Glossary 2012 shall apply and, unless the context otherwise requires:

(a) all italicised terms shall be defined; and

(b) all terms shall be interpreted,

in accordance with the *Glossary*.

Rule 49: Interest

[Deleted]

Rule 50: Accounts

[Deleted]

Rule 50A: Client money

50A.1 You must comply with this Part if you have held or received *client money*.

50A.2 In all dealings with *client money*, you must:

(a) keep *client money* separate from money which is not *client money*;

(b) on receipt, pay *client money* into a *client account* without undue delay and keep it there, unless the *client* has agreed otherwise, or it is paid directly to a third party in the execution of a *trust* under which it is held;

(c) ensure by use of proper accounting systems and processes that *client money* is used for *client's* matters only and for the purposes for which it has been paid;

(d) use money held as *trustee* of a *trust* for the purposes of that *trust* only;

(e) establish and maintain proper accounting systems and proper internal controls over those systems to ensure compliance with these rules;

(f) return *client money* to the person on whose behalf the money is held promptly, as soon as there is no longer any proper reason to retain those funds;

(g) keep accounting records to show accurately the position with regard to the money held for each *client* and *trust* for a minimum period of six years;

(h) Account for interest on *client money* in accordance with rule 22.

Rule 50B: Accountants' Reports

50B.1 You must obtain an accountant's report in respect of any period during which you or the *Exempt European Practice* from which you practice have held or received *client money* unless you fall within any of the exceptions contained in rule 32A.1A.

50B.2 You must comply with the rules in Part 6 in relation to any accountant's report that you are required to obtain under rule 50B.1.

Rule 51: Production of documents, information and explanations

51.1 You must promptly comply with:

(a) a written notice from the *SRA* that you must produce for inspection by the appointee of the *SRA* all documents held by you or held under your control and all information and explanations requested:

(i) in connection with your practice; or

(ii) in connection with any *trust* of which you are, or formerly were, a *trustee*;

for the purpose of ascertaining whether any person subject to Part 7 of these rules is complying with or has complied with any provision of this Part of these rules, or on whether the account has been used for or in connection with a breach of any of the Principles or other SRA Handbook requirements made or issued by the *SRA*; and

(b) a notice given by the *SRA* in accordance with section 44B or 44BA of the *SA* or section 93 of the *LSA* for the provision of documents, information or explanations.

51.2 You must provide any necessary permissions for information to be given so as to enable the appointee of the *SRA* to:

(a) prepare a report on the documents produced under rule 51.1 above; and

(b) seek verification from clients, staff and the banks, building societies or other financial institutions used by you.

51.3 You must comply with all requests from the *SRA* or its appointee as to:

(a) the form in which you produce any documents you hold electronically; and

(b) photocopies of any documents to take away.

51.4 A notice under this rule is deemed to be duly served:

(a) on the date on which it is delivered to or left at your address;

(b) on the date on which it is sent electronically to your e-mail or fax address; or

(c) 48 hours (excluding Saturdays, Sundays and Bank Holidays) after it has been sent by post or document exchange to your last notified practising address.

Rule 52: Waivers

52.1 The *SRA* may waive in writing in any particular case or cases any of the provisions of Part 7 of the rules, may place conditions on, and may revoke, any waiver.

Guidance note

(i) Applications for waivers should be made to the Professional Ethics Guidance Team. You will need to show that your circumstances are exceptional in order for a waiver to be granted.

PART 8:

[Deleted]

APPENDIX 1: FLOWCHART – EFFECT OF SRA ACCOUNTS RULES 2011

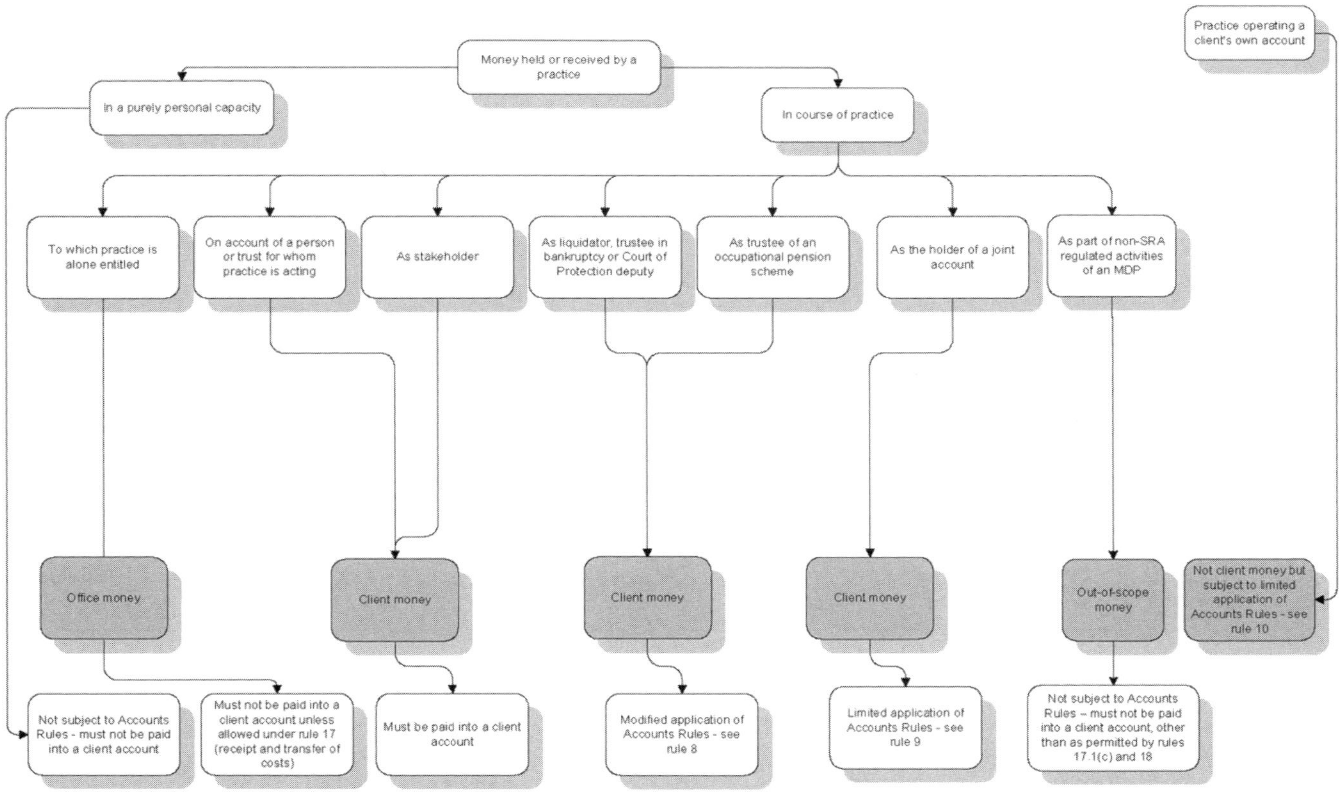

APPENDIX 2: SPECIAL SITUATIONS – WHAT APPLIES

		Is it client money?	Subject to reconcilia-tions?	Keep books?	Retain state-ments?	Subject to account-ant's report?	Produce records to SRA?	Interest?	Retain records gen-erally?	Central records?	Subject to reporting account-ant's compari-sons?
1	R.15.1(a) a/cs in practice name (not client a/c)	Yes	Yes	Yes – r.29.1(a) and 29.2	Yes – r.29.17	Yes	Yes	Yes – r.22	Yes – r.29.17	Statem-ents or register – r.29.19, bills – r.29.15	Yes – r.39.1(f)
2	R.15.1(b) a/cs in name of client – not operated by practice	No	No	No – record receipt and payment only	No	No	No	No – all interest earned for client – r.22, guidance note (i)(i)	No – except record of receipt and payment	Bills – r.29.15	No
3	R.15.1(b) a/cs in name of client – operated by practice	No	No	No – record receipt and payment only	Yes – r.30	Limited – r.39.1(n)	Yes – r.10	No – all interest earned for client – r.22, guidance note (i)(i)	No – except record of receipt and payment	State-ments – r.30, Bills – r.29.15	No

		Is it client money?	Subject to reconciliations?	Keep books?	Retain statements?	Subject to accountant's report?	Produce records to SRA?	Interest?	Retain records generally?	Central records?	Subject to reporting accountant's comparisons?
4	Liquidators, trustees in bankruptcy and Court of Protection deputies	Yes – r.8	No – r.8	Modified – statutory records – r.8	Yes – r.8 and r.29.17(c)	Limited – r.39.1(l)	Yes – r.8	No – r.8 – comply with statutory rules (but see r.8.4 and r.22, guidance note (iv)(a))	Yes – modified r.29.17(c)	Yes – r.29.20 Bills – r.29.15	No – r.8
5	Trustees of occupational pension schemes	Yes – r.8	No – r.8	Modified – statutory records – r.8	Yes – r.8 and r.29.17(c)	Limited – r.39.1(l)	Yes – r.8	No – r.8 – comply with statutory rules (but see r.8.4 and r.22, guidance note (iv)(a))	Yes – modified r.29.17(c)	Yes – r.29.20 Bills – r.29.15	No – r.8

		Is it client money?	Subject to reconciliations?	Keep books?	Retain statements?	Subject to accountant's report?	Produce records to SRA?	Interest?	Retain records generally?	Central records?	Subject to reporting accountant's comparisons?
6	Joint accounts – r.9	Yes – r.9	No – r.9	No – r.9	Yes – r.9 and 29.17 (b)(ii)	Limited – r.39.1(m)	Yes – r.9	No. For joint a/c with client, all interest to client (r.22, guidance note (v)(a)); for joint a/c with another practice or other third party, depends on agreement	No – r.9	Statements – r.29.21 Bills – r.29.15	No – r.9
7	Acting under power of attorney	Yes	Yes	Yes	Yes	Yes	Yes	Yes	Yes	Bills – r.29.15	Yes

		Is it client money?	Subject to reconciliations?	Keep books?	Retain statements?	Subject to accountant's report?	Produce records to SRA?	Interest?	Retain records generally?	Central records?	Subject to reporting accountant's comparisons?
8	Operating client's own a/c e.g. under power of attorney – r.10	No	No	No	Yes – r.30	Limited – r.39.1(n)	Yes – r.10	No – all interest earned for client (r.22, guidance note (i)(i))	No – r.10	Statements – r.30 Bills – r.29.15	No
9	Exempt persons under r.5	No	No	No	No	No	No	No	No	No	No
10	Non-SRA regulated activities of an MDP	No – out-of-scope money – r.12	No	No – but see guidance note (xi) to r.29	No	No	Yes – r.31 – only to extent needed to check rule compliance	No	No – but see guidance note (xi) to r.29	No	No

APPENDIX 3: SRA GUIDELINES – ACCOUNTING PROCEDURES AND SYSTEMS

1. Introduction

1.1 These guidelines, published under rule 26 of the SRA Accounts Rules 2011, are intended to be a benchmark or broad statement of good practice requirements which should be present in an effective regime for the proper control of client money. They should therefore be of positive assistance to firms in establishing or reviewing appropriate procedures and systems. They do not override, or detract from the need to comply fully with, the Accounts Rules.

1.2 References to managers or firms in the guidelines are intended to include sole practitioners, recognised bodies and licensed bodies, and the managers of those bodies.

2. General

2.1 Compliance with the Accounts Rules is the equal responsibility of all managers in a firm. This responsibility also extends to the Compliance Officer for Finance and Administration, whether or not a manager (see rule 6). They should establish policies and systems to ensure that the firm complies fully with the rules, including procedures for verifying that the controls are operating effectively. Responsibility for day to day supervision may be delegated to one or more managers to enable effective control to be exercised. Delegation of total responsibility to a cashier or book-keeper is not acceptable.

2.2 The firm should hold a copy of the current version of the Accounts Rules and/or have ready access to the current on-line version. The person who maintains the books of account must have a full knowledge of the requirements of the rules and the accounting requirements of firms.

2.3 Proper books of account should be maintained on the double-entry principle. They should be legible, up to date and contain narratives with the entries which identify and/or provide adequate information about the transaction. Entries should be made in chronological order and the current balance should be shown on client ledger accounts, or be readily ascertainable, in accordance with rule 29.9.

2.4 Ledger accounts for clients, other persons or trusts should include the name of the client or other person or trust and contain a heading which provides a description of the matter or transaction.

2.5 Manual systems for recording client money are capable of complying with these guidelines. A computer system, with suitable support procedures will, however, provide an efficient means of producing the accounts and associated control information.

2.6 When introducing new systems, care must be taken to ensure:

(1) that balances transferred from the books of account of the old system are reconciled with the opening balances held on the new system before day to day operation commences;

(2) that the new system operates correctly before the old system is abandoned. This may require a period of parallel running of the old and new systems and the satisfactory reconciliation of the two sets of records before the old system ceases.

2.7 The firm should ensure that office account entries in relation to each client or trust matter are maintained up to date as well as the client account entries. Credit balances on office account in respect of client or trust matters should be fully investigated.

2.8 The firm should establish policies and operate systems for the payment of fair and reasonable interest to clients in accordance with rules 22 and 23.

3. Receipt of client money

3.1 The firm should have procedures for identifying client money, including cash, when received in the firm, and for promptly recording the receipt of the money either in the books of account or a register for later posting to the client cash book and ledger accounts. The procedures should cover money received through the post, electronically or direct by fee earners or other personnel. They should also cover the safekeeping of money prior to payment to bank.

3.2 The firm should have a system which ensures that client money is paid promptly into a client account.

3.3 The firm should have a system for identifying money which should not be in a client account and for transferring it without delay.

3.4 The firm should determine a policy and operate a system for dealing with money which is a mixture of office money and client money, or client money and out-of-scope money, or client money, out-of-scope money and office money, in compliance with rules 17–19.

4. Payments from client account

4.1 The firm should have clear procedures for ensuring that all withdrawals from client accounts are properly authorised. In particular, suitable persons should be named for the following purposes:

(1) authorisation of internal payment vouchers;

(2) signing client account cheques;

(3) authorising telegraphic or electronic transfers.

No other personnel should be allowed to authorise or sign the documents.

4.2 The firm should establish clear procedures and systems for ensuring that persons permitted to authorise the withdrawal of client money from a client account have an appropriate understanding of the requirements of the rules, including rules 20 and 21 which set out when and how a withdrawal from client account may properly be made.

4.3 Persons nominated for the purpose of authorising internal payment vouchers should, for each payment, ensure there is supporting evidence showing clearly the reason for the payment, and the date of it. Similarly, persons signing cheques and authorising transfers should ensure there is a suitable voucher or other supporting evidence to support the payment.

4.4 The firm should have clear systems and procedures for authorising withdrawals from client accounts by electronic means, with appropriate safeguards and controls to ensure that all such withdrawals are properly authorised.

4.5 The firm should have a system for checking the balances on client ledger accounts to ensure no debit balances occur. Where payments are to be made other than out of cleared funds, clear policies and procedures must be in place to ensure that adequate risk assessment is applied.

N.B. If incoming payments are ultimately dishonoured, a debit balance will arise, in breach of the rules, and full replacement of the shortfall will be required under rule 7. See also rule 20, guidance notes (iii)(a) and (iv)(a).

4.6 The firm should establish systems for the transfer of costs from client account to office account in accordance with rule 17.2 and 17.3. Normally transfers should be made only on the basis of rendering a bill or written notification. The payment from the client account should be by way of a cheque or transfer in favour of the firm or sole principal – see rule 21.4.

4.7 The firm should establish policies and operate systems to control and record accurately any transfers between clients of the firm. Where these arise as a result of loans between clients, the written authority of both the lender and borrower must be obtained in accordance with rule 27.2.

4.8 The firm should establish policies and operate systems for the timely closure of files, and the prompt accounting for surplus balances in accordance with rule 14.3.

4.9 The firm should establish systems in accordance with rule 14.4 to keep clients (or other people on whose behalf money is held) regularly informed when funds are retained for a specified reason at the end of a matter or the substantial conclusion of a matter.

5. Overall control of client accounts

5.1 The firm should maintain control of all its bank and building society accounts opened for the purpose of holding client money. In the case of a joint account, a suitable degree of control should be exercised.

5.2 Central records or central registers must be kept in respect of:

(1) accounts held for client money, which are not client accounts (rules 15.1(a), 16.1(d) and 29.19);

(2) practice as a liquidator, trustee in bankruptcy, Court of Protection deputy or trustee of an occupational pension scheme (rules 8 and 29.20);

(3) joint accounts (rules 9 and 29.21);

(4) dividend payments received by an executor, trustee or nominee company as nominee (rules 28.2 and 29.23); and

(5) clients' own accounts (rules 10, 15.1(b) and 30.3).

5.3 In addition, there should be a master list of all:

- general client accounts;
- separate designated client accounts;
- accounts held in respect of 5.2 above; and
- office accounts.

The master list should show the current status of each account; e.g. currently in operation or closed with date of closure.

5.4 The firm should operate a system to ensure that accurate reconciliations of the client accounts are carried out at least every five weeks. In particular it should ensure that:

(1) a full list of client ledger balances is produced. Any debit balances should be listed, fully investigated and rectified immediately. The total of any debit balances cannot be "netted off" against the total of credit balances;

(2) a full list of unpresented cheques is produced;

(3) a list of outstanding lodgements is produced;

(4) formal statements are produced reconciling the client account cash book balances, aggregate client ledger balances and the client bank accounts. All unresolved differences must be investigated and, where appropriate, corrective action taken;

(5) a manager or the Compliance Officer for Finance and Administration checks the reconciliation statement and any corrective action, and ensures that enquiries are made into any unusual or apparently unsatisfactory items or still unresolved matters.

5.5 The firm should have clear policies, systems and procedures to control access to computerised client accounts by determining the personnel who should have "write to" and "read only" access. Passwords should be held confidentially by designated personnel and changed regularly to maintain security. Access to the system should not unreasonably be restricted to a single person nor should more people than necessary be given access.

5.6 The firm should establish policies and systems for the retention of the accounting records to ensure:

- books of account, reconciliations, bills, bank statements and passbooks are kept for at least six years;
- paid cheques, digital images of paid cheques and other authorities for the withdrawal of money from a client account are kept for at least two years;
- other vouchers and internal expenditure authorisation documents relating directly to entries in the client account books are kept for at least two years.

5.7 The firm should ensure that unused client account cheques are stored securely to prevent unauthorised access. Blank cheques should not be pre-signed. Any cancelled cheques should be retained.

APPENDIX 4: REPORTING ACCOUNTANT'S CHECKLIST

[Any checks made in respect of the period [ ] to 5 October 2011 relate to compliance with the Solicitors' Accounts Rules 1998.]

The following items have been tested to satisfy the examination requirements under rules 38-40, with the results as indicated. Where the position has been found to be unsatisfactory as a result of these tests, further details have been reported in section 6 of this checklist or reported by separate appendix.

Name of practice	

Results of test checks:

1. For all client money		Were any breaches discovered? (Tick the appropriate column.)		If "yes" should breaches be noted in the accountant;'s report?		Cross reference to audit file documentation.
(a)	**Book-keeping system for every office:**	Yes	No	Yes	No	
(i)	The accounting records satisfactorily distinguish client money from all other money dealt with by the firm.					
(ii)	A separate ledger account is maintained for each client and trust (excepting section (l) below) and the particulars of all client money received, held or paid on account of each client and trust, including funds held on separate designated deposits, or elsewhere, are recorded.					
(iii)	The client ledgers for clients and trusts show a current balance at all times, or the current balance is readily ascertainable.					
(iv)	A record of all bills of costs and written notifications has been maintained, either in the form of a central record or a file of copies of such bills.					
(b)	**Postings to ledger accounts and casts:**	Yes	No	Yes	No	
(i)	Postings to ledger accounts for clients and trusts from records of receipts and payments are correct.					
(ii)	Casts of ledger accounts for clients and trusts and receipts and payments records are correct.					
(iii)	Postings have been recorded in chronological sequence with the date being that of the initiation of the transaction.					
(c)	**Receipts and payments of client money:**	Yes	No	Yes	No	
(i)	Sample receipts and payments of client money as shown in bank and building society statements have been compared with the firm's records of receipts and payments of client money, and are correct.					

16/09/2011 Page 1 of 5 www.sra.org.uk

For alternative formats, email info.services@sra.org.uk or telephone 0870 606 2555.

1. continued…..		Were any breaches discovered? (Tick the appropriate column.)		If "yes" should breaches be noted in the accountant;'s report?		Cross reference to audit file documentation.
(ii)	Sample paid cheques, or digital images of the front and back of sample paid cheques, have been obtained and details agreed to receipts and payment records.					
(d)	**System of recording costs and making transfers:**	Yes	No	Yes	No	
(i)	The firm's system of recording costs has been ascertained and is suitable.					
(ii)	Costs have been drawn only where required for or towards payment of the firm's costs where there has been sent to the client a bill of costs or other written notification of the amount of the costs.					
(e)	**Examination of documents for verification of transactions and entries in accounting records:**	Yes	No	Yes	No	
(i)	Make a test examination of a number of client and trust files.					
(ii)	All client and trust files requested for examination were made available.					
(iii)	The financial transactions as detailed on client and trust files and other documentation (including transfers from one ledger account to another) were valid and appropriately authorised in accordance with Parts 1 and 2 of the SRA Accounts Rules 2011 (AR).					
(iv)	The financial transactions evidenced by documents on the client and trust files were correctly recorded in the books of account in a manner complying with Part 4 AR.					
(f)	**Extraction of client ledger balances for clients and trusts:**	Yes	No	Yes	No	
(i)	The extraction of client ledger balances for clients and trusts has been checked for no fewer than two separate dates in the period subject to this report.					
(ii)	The total liabilities to clients and trusts as shown by such ledger accounts has been compared to the cash account balance(s) at each of the separate dates selected in (f)(i) above and agreed.					
(iii)	The cash account balance(s) at each of the dates selected has/have been reconciled to the balance(s) in client bank account and elsewhere as confirmed directly by the relevant banks and building societies.					
(g)	**Reconciliations:**	Yes	No	Yes	No	
(i)	During the accounting year under review, reconciliations have been carried out at least every five weeks.					
(ii)	Each reconciliation is in the form of a statement set out in a logical format which is likely to reveal any discrepancies.					
(iii)	Reconciliation statements have been retained.					
(iv)	On entries in an appropriate sample of reconciliation statements:	Yes	No	Yes	No	
	(A) All accounts containing client money have been included.					
	(B) All ledger account balances for clients and trusts as at the reconciliation date have been listed and totalled. (C) No debit balances on ledger accounts for clients and trusts have been included in the total.					

16/09/2011 Page 2 of 5 www.sra.org.uk

1. continued…….	Were any breaches discovered? (Tick the appropriate column.)		If "yes" should breaches be noted in the accountant's report?		Cross reference to audit file documentation.
(D) The cash account balance(s) for clients and trusts is/are correctly calculated by the accurate and up to date recording of transactions.					
(E) The client bank account totals for clients and trusts are complete and correct being calculated by:					
the closing balance ***plus*** an accurate and complete list of outstanding lodgements ***less*** an accurate and complete list of unpresented cheques.					
(v) Each reconciliation selected under paragraph (iv) above has been achieved by the comparison and agreement ***without adjusting or balancing entries*** of: total of ledger balances for clients and trusts; total of cash account balances for clients and trusts; total of client bank accounts.					
(vi) In the event of debit balances existing on ledger accounts for clients and trusts, the firm has investigated promptly and corrected the position satisfactorily.					
(vii) In the event of the reconciliations selected under paragraph (iv) above not being in agreement, the differences have been investigated and corrected promptly.					
(h) Payments of client money:	Yes	No	Yes	No	
Make a test examination of the ledger accounts for clients and trusts in order to ascertain whether payments have been made on any individual account in excess of money held on behalf of that client or trust.					
(i) Office accounts - client money:	Yes	No	Yes	No	
(i) Check such office ledger and cash account and bank and building society statements as the firm maintains with a view to ascertaining whether any client money has not been paid into a client account.					
(ii) Investigate office ledger credit balances and ensure that such balances do not include client money incorrectly held in office account.					
(j) Client money not held in client account:	Yes	No	Yes	No	
(i) Have sums not held on client account been identified?					
(ii) Has the reason for holding such sums outside client account been established?					
(iii) Has a written client agreement been made if appropriate?					
(iv) Are central records or a central register kept for client money held outside client account on the client's instructions?					
(k) Rule 27 - inter-client transfers:	Yes	No	Yes	No	
Make test checks of inter-client transfers to ensure that rule 27 has been complied with.					
(l) Rule 29.10 - acting for borrower and lender:	Yes	No	Yes	No	
Make a test examination of the client ledger accounts in order to ascertain whether rule 29.10 AR has been complied with, where the firm acts for both borrower and lender in a conveyancing transaction.					
(m) Rule 29.23 – executor, trustee or nominee companies:	Yes	No	Yes	No	
Is a central book of dividend instruction letters kept?					

16/09/2011 Page 3 of 5 www.sra.org.uk

1. continued…….		Were any breaches discovered? (Tick the appropriate column.)		If 'yes' should breaches be noted in the accountant's report?		Cross reference to audit file documentation.
(n)	**Information and explanations:**	Yes	No	Yes	No	
	All information and explanations required have been received and satisfactorily cleared.					

2.	Liquidators, trustees in bankruptcy, Court of Protection deputies and trustees of occupational pension schemes (rule 8)	Were any breaches discovered? (Tick the appropriate column.)		If 'yes' should breaches be noted in the accountant's report?		Cross reference to audit file documentation
		Yes	No	Yes	No	
(a)	A record of all bills of costs and written notifications has been maintained, either in the form of a central record or a file of copies of such bills or notifications.					
(b)	Records kept under rule 8 including any statements, passbooks and other accounting records originating outside the firm's office have been retained.					
(c)	Records kept under rule 8 are kept together centrally, or a central register is kept of the appointments.					

3.	Joint accounts (rule 9)	Were any breaches discovered? (Tick the appropriate column.)		If 'yes' should breaches be noted in the accountant's report?		Cross reference to audit file documentation
		Yes	No	Yes	No	
(a)	A record of all bills of costs and written notifications has been maintained, either in the form of a central record or a file of copies of such bills or notifications.					
(b)	Statements and passbooks and/or duplicate statements or copies of passbook entries have been retained.					
(c)	Statements, passbooks, duplicate statements and copies of passbook entries are kept together centrally, or a central register of all joint accounts is kept.					

4.	Clients' own accounts (rule 10)	Were any breaches discovered? (Tick the appropriate column.)		If 'yes' should breaches be noted in the accountant's report?		Cross reference to audit file documentation
		Yes	No	Yes	No	
(a)	Statements and passbooks and/or duplicate statements, copies of passbook entries and cheque details have been retained					
(b)	Statements and passbooks and/or duplicate statements, copies of passbook entries and cheque details are kept together centrally, or a central register of clients' own accounts is kept.					

16/09/2011 Page 4 of 5 www.sra.org.uk

5.	SRA guidelines - accounting procedures and systems		
		Yes	No
	Discovery of substantial departures from the guidelines? *If "yes" please give details below.*		

6. Please give further details of unsatisfactory items below. (Please attach additional schedules as required.)

Signature	Date
Reporting Accountant	Print Name

APPENDIX 5: ACCOUNTANT'S REPORT FORM[1]

AR1 - Accountant's Report Form

Solicitors Regulation Authority

The circumstances in which an annual Accountant's Report is required to be obtained and delivered to us are set out in Rule 32 of the SRA Accounts Rules 2011 (the Rules). For further information on the Rules and for clarification on whether or not the requirement to deliver an Accountant's Report applies to you, see our website at http://www.sra.org.uk/solicitors/handbook/accountsrules/content.page.

This Report must be completed by the Accountant within 6 months of the end of the Accounting Period to which the Report relates.

The Accountant who prepares the Report must be qualified under Rule 34 of the Rules.

The Accountant should have read carefully the separate Guidance www.sra.org.uk/ar1 we have issued before commencing the programme of work which will enable completion of this Report. The Guidance provides useful information as to which Rules are covered by this Report, the areas and types of work they should be considering and the factors that might lead to qualification of this report.

When a practice closes but the ceased practice continues to hold or receive client money during the process of dealing with outstanding costs and unattributable or unreturnable funds, the Rules, including the obligation to deliver Accountant's Reports, will continue to apply.

When a practice ceases to hold and/or receive client money (and/or to operate any client's own account as signatory), either on closure of the practice or for any other reason, the practice must obtain and deliver a final report within 6 months of ceasing to hold and/or receive client money (and/or to operate any client's own account as signatory), whether qualified or not, unless we require earlier delivery.

If you need any assistance completing this Report, please telephone the Contact Centre on 0370 606 2555. Our lines are open from 08.00 to 18.00 Monday, Wednesday, Thursday, Friday and 09.30 to 18.00 Tuesday. Please note calls may be monitored/recorded for training purposes.

If you are calling from overseas please use +44 (0) 121 329 6800. Note that reports in respect of practice from an office outside England and Wales are submitted under Part 7 of the Rules. Specimen form **AR2** may be used for such reports.

Section 1 - Firm details

Insert here all names used by the firm or in-house practice from the offices covered by this Report. This must include the registered name of a recognised body/licensed body which is an LLP or company, and the name under which a partnership or sole practitioner is recognised. It is assumed that all addresses used by the practice during the accounting period are covered by this report, except offices outside England and Wales (Refer to Part 7 of the Rules). All addresses of the practice during the reporting period must be covered by an Accountant's Report.

Firm name(s) during the reporting period:		SRA No:	
Report Period From:		to	

1. Last updated 21 October 2015. This form of report is for use by all firms whose next accounting period ends on or after 1 November 2015. SRA guidance on completing the form appears at **6.4**. Transitional arrangements mean that firms with an accounting period end date before 1 November 2015 comply with the requirements for accountants' reports in version 14 of the SRA Accounts Rules 2011 (see **www.sra.org.uk**). The reporting accountant will use that version of the reporting accountant's checklist at Appendix 4, and the form of report at Appendix 5.

Firm COFA(s) (if more than one) during the reporting period: ☐

☐

COFA's SRA/CRM No: ☐

☐

Dates of appointment (where appropriate): ☐ to ☐

Is this a cease to hold Report? Yes ☐ No ☐

If **YES**: this report should be submitted to the SRA by the firm whether qualified or not.

Have any consultants or employees held or received client money, or operated a client's own account as signatory, during the report period? Yes ☐ No ☐

If **YES**: please set out the details on a separate sheet of paper if necessary.

Section 2 - Work undertaken and declarations

1. We confirm that we are qualified to prepare this Report in accordance with Rule 34 of the SRA Accounts Rules 2011.

2. We confirm that a copy of this Report has been sent to the firm's current COFA as set out in Section 1 of this Report.

3. We confirm that we have carried out work to assess whether the firm has complied with the relevant Accounts Rules, in the period covered by this Report, namely – Rules 1, 7, 13, 14, 17, 18, 20, 21, 27 and 29 and also Rules 8, 9, 10, 15, 16 and 19 where applicable.

   We have considered the SRA's guidance and have found material breaches of the Accounts Rules (as set out in 3 above), and/or significant weaknesses in the firm's systems and controls for compliance with the Accounts Rules (as set out in 3 above). We therefore consider that the SRA should be notified by our qualifying this Report. Yes ☐ No ☐

   If **YES:** then this Report should be submitted to the SRA and all matters of significance should be detailed in the box below.

☐

Page 2 AR1 v8 21.10.15

Section 3 - Accountant's details and signature

Name of Accountant: [ ]

Professional body: [ ]

Accountant membership/ registration number: [ ]

Recognised Supervisory Body under which individual/firm is a registered auditor:

[ ]

Reference number of individual/firm audit registration(s):

[ ]

Firm name: [ ]

Firm address: [ ]

[ ]

[ ]

Email address: [ ]

Signature of Accountant: [ ] Date: [ ]

[ ] If completed electronically please tick to say you confirm the declaration

Once completed this Report should be returned by the firm within the time period required by the Rules via one of the options below:

Email: SRAAccountantsReports@sra.org.uk

Post: Authorisation – Accountant's Reports
Solicitors Regulation Authority
The Cube
199 Wharfside Street
Birmingham
B1 1RN

DX: DX 720293 Birmingham 47

These reports should be retained by both the firm and by the Reporting Accountant for at least 6 years, regardless of whether submitted to the SRA.

Page 3 AR1 v8 21.10.15

[2] SRA Principles, Code of Conduct and Overseas Rules

[2.1] SRA Principles 2011 (extracts)

[Last updated 1 November 2015]

PREAMBLE

The SRA Principles dated 17 June 2011 commencing 6 October 2011 made by the Solicitors Regulation Authority Board under sections 31, 79 and 80 of the Solicitors Act 1974, sections 9 and 9A of the Administration of Justice Act 1985 and section 83 of the Legal Services Act 2007, with the approval of the Legal Services Board under paragraph 19 of Schedule 4 to the Legal Services Act 2007, regulating the conduct of solicitors and their employees, registered European lawyers, recognised bodies and their managers and employees, and licensed bodies and their managers and employees.

PART 1: SRA PRINCIPLES

1: SRA Principles

These are mandatory *Principles* which apply to all.

You must:

1. uphold the rule of law and the proper administration of justice;

2. act with integrity;

3. not allow your independence to be compromised;

4. act in the best interests of each *client*;

5. provide a proper standard of service to your *clients*;

6. behave in a way that maintains the trust the public places in you and in the provision of legal services;

7. comply with your legal and regulatory obligations and deal with your regulators and ombudsmen in an open, timely and co-operative manner;

8. run your business or carry out your role in the business effectively and in accordance with proper governance and sound financial and risk management principles;

9. run your business or carry out your role in the business in a way that encourages equality of opportunity and respect for diversity; and

10. protect *client* money and *assets*.

2: SRA Principles – notes

2.1 The Principles embody the key ethical requirements on firms and individuals who are involved in the provision of legal services. You should always have regard to the Principles and use them as your starting point when faced with an ethical dilemma.

2.2 Where two or more Principles come into conflict, the Principle which takes precedence is the one which best serves the public interest in the particular circumstances, especially the public interest in the proper administration of justice.

2.3 These Principles:

(a) apply to individuals and firms we regulate, whether traditional firms of solicitors or ABSs, in private practice or in-house. Where a firm or individual is *practising overseas*, the Overseas Principles apply;

(b) will be breached by you if you permit another person to do anything on your behalf which if done by you would breach the Principles; and

(c) apply to you to the fullest extent if a sole practitioner or manager in a firm, but still apply to you if you work within a firm or in-house and have no management responsibility (for example, even if you are not a manager you may have an opportunity to influence, adopt and implement measures to comply with Principles 8 and 9).

2.4 Compliance with the Principles is also subject to any overriding legal obligations.

Principle 1: You must uphold the rule of law and the proper administration of justice.

2.5 You have obligations not only to clients but also to the court and to third parties with whom you have dealings on your clients' behalf – see, e.g., Chapter 5 (Your client and the court) and Chapter 11 (Relations with third parties) of the Code.

Principle 2: You must act with integrity.

2.6 Personal integrity is central to your role as the client's trusted adviser and should characterise all your professional dealings with clients, the court, other lawyers and the public.

Principle 3: You must not allow your independence to be compromised.

2.7 "Independence" means your own and your firm's independence, and not merely your ability to give independent advice to a client. You should avoid situations which might put your independence at risk – e.g. giving control of your practice to a third party which is beyond the regulatory reach of the SRA or other approved regulator.

Principle 4: You must act in the best interests of each client.

2.8 You should always act in good faith and do your best for each of your clients. Most importantly, you should observe:

(a) your duty of confidentiality to the client – see Chapter 4 (Confidentiality and disclosure) of the Code; and

(b) your obligations with regard to conflicts of interests – see Chapter 3 (Conflicts of interests) of the Code.

Principle 5: You must provide a proper standard of service to your clients.

2.9 You should, e.g., provide a proper standard of client care and of work. This would include exercising competence, skill and diligence, and taking into account the individual needs and circumstances of each client.

2.10 For a *solicitor*, meeting the competencies set out in the Competence Statement forms an integral part of the requirement to provide a proper standard of service.

Principle 6: You must behave in a way that maintains the trust the public places in you and in the provision of legal services.

2.11 Members of the public should be able to place their trust in you. Any behaviour either within or outside your professional practice which undermines this trust damages not only you, but also the ability of the legal profession as a whole to serve society.

Principle 7: You must comply with your legal and regulatory obligations and deal with your regulators and ombudsmen in an open, timely and co-operative manner.

2.12 You should, e.g., ensure that you comply with all the reporting and notification requirements – see Chapter 10 (You and your regulator) of the Code – and respond promptly and substantively to communications.

Principle 8: You must run your business or carry out your role in the business effectively and in accordance with proper governance and sound financial and risk management principles.

2.13 Whether you are a manager or an employee, you have a part to play in helping to ensure that your business is well run for the benefit of your clients and, e.g. in meeting the outcomes in Chapter 7 (Management of your business) of the Code.

Principle 9: You must run your business or carry out your role in the business in a way that encourages equality of opportunity and respect for diversity.

2.14 Whether you are a manager or an employee, you have a role to play in achieving the outcomes in Chapter 2 (Equality and diversity) of the Code. Note that a finding of unlawful discrimination outside practice could also amount to a breach of Principles 1 and 6.

Principle 10: You must protect client money and assets.

2.15 This Principle goes to the heart of the duty to act in the best interests of your clients. You should play your part in e.g. protecting money, documents or other property belonging to your clients which has been entrusted to you or your firm.

Breach of the Principles

2.16 Our approach to enforcement is proportionate, outcomes-focused and risk-based. Therefore, how we deal with failure to comply with the Principles will depend on all the particular circumstances of each case. Our primary aim is to achieve the right outcomes for clients.

PART 2: SRA PRINCIPLES – APPLICATION PROVISIONS

The *Principles* apply to you in the following circumstances (and "you" must be construed accordingly).

3: Application of the SRA Principles in England and Wales

3.1 Subject to paragraphs 3.2 to 6.1 below and any other provisions in the *SRA Code of Conduct*, the *Principles* apply to you, in relation to your activities carried out from an office in England and Wales, if you are:

- (a) a *solicitor*, *REL* or *RFL* who is *practising* as such, whether or not the entity through which you *practise* is subject to these *Principles*;
- (b) a *solicitor*, *REL* or *RFL* who is:
  - (i) a *manager*, *employee* or *owner* of a body which should be a *recognised body*, but has not been recognised by the *SRA*;
  - (ii) a *manager*, *employee* or *owner* of a body that is a *manager* or *owner* of a body that should be a *recognised body*, but has not been recognised by the *SRA*;
  - (iii) an *employee* in a *sole practitioner's practice* which should be a *recognised sole practice*, but has not been recognised by the *SRA*;
  - (iv) an *owner* of an *authorised body* or of a body which should be a *recognised body* but has not been recognised by the *SRA*, even if you undertake no work for the body's *clients*;
  - (v) a *manager* or *employee* of an *authorised non-SRA firm*, or a *manager* of a body which is a *manager* of an *authorised non-SRA firm*, when doing work of a sort authorised by the *SRA*, for that firm;
- (c) an *authorised body*, or a body which should be a *recognised body* but has not been recognised by the *SRA*;
- (d) any other person who is a *manager*, or *employee* of an *authorised body*, or of a body which should be a *recognised body* but has not been recognised by the *SRA*;

(e) any other person who is an *employee* in a *recognised sole practice*, or of a *sole practitioner* whose *practice* should be a *recognised sole practice*, but has not been recognised by the *SRA*;

and "you" includes "your" as appropriate.

3.2 The *Principles* apply to you if you are a *solicitor*, *REL* or *RFL*, and you are:

(a) *practising* as a *manager* or *employee* of an *authorised non-SRA firm* when doing work of a sort authorised by the *authorised non-SRA firm's approved regulator* or carrying on any other activity that is not precluded by the terms of your authorisation from the firm's *approved regulator*; or

(b) an *owner* of an *authorised non-SRA firm* even if you undertake no work for the body's *clients*.

3.3 The *Principles* apply to you if you are an *REL practising* as a *manager*, *employee*, *member* or *interest holder*, of an *Exempt European Practice*.

4: Application of the SRA Principles in relation to practice from an office outside England and Wales

4.1 The *Principles* apply to you if you are:

(a) a body practising from an office outside England and Wales only if you are required to be an *authorised body* as a result of the nature of your practice and you have been authorised by the *SRA* accordingly; or

(b) a *manager* of such a body.

Guidance note

(i) In most circumstances, overseas offices of authorised bodies based in England and Wales will not require authorisation with the SRA and will be governed by the SRA Overseas Rules. However, in some circumstances, because of the work that is being carried out from the overseas office, it will need to be authorised (see Rule 2.1(e) and have regard to Rule 2.1(g) of the SRA Overseas Rules). In those circumstances, the SRA Principles and Code of Conduct apply.

4.2 The *Principles* apply to you if you are an individual engaged in *temporary practice overseas*.

5: Application of the SRA Principles outside practice

5.1 In relation to activities which fall outside *practice*, whether undertaken as a *lawyer* or in some other business or private capacity, *Principles* 1, 2 and 6 apply to you if you are a *solicitor*, *REL* or *RFL*.

6: General provisions

6.1 You must comply with the *Principles* at all times, but the extent to which you are expected to implement the requirements of the *Principles* will depend on your role in the *firm*, or your way of *practising*. For example, those who are managing a business will be expected to have more influence on how the *firm* or business is run than those *practising* in-house but not managing a legal department, or those *practising* as *employees* of a *firm*.

PART 3: TRANSITIONAL PROVISIONS

7: Transitional provisions

7.1 For the avoidance of doubt, where a breach of any provision of the Solicitors' Code of Conduct 2007 comes to the attention of the *SRA* after 6 October 2011, this shall be subject to action by the *SRA* notwithstanding any repeal of the relevant provision.

7.2 [Deleted]

7.3 [Deleted]

7.4 [Deleted]

PART 4: INTERPRETATION

8: Interpretation

8.1 The SRA Handbook Glossary 2012 shall apply to these rules and, unless the context otherwise requires:

(a) all italicised terms within these rules shall be defined; and

(b) terms within these rules shall be interpreted,

in accordance with the *Glossary*.

[2.2] SRA Code of Conduct 2011 (extracts)

[Last updated 1 April 2016]

2ND SECTION: YOU AND YOUR BUSINESS

Chapter 7: Management of your business

This chapter is about the management and supervision of your *firm* or *in-house practice*.

Everyone has a role to play in the efficient running of a business, although of course that role will depend on the individual's position within the organisation. However, overarching responsibility for the management of the business in the broadest sense rests with the *manager(s)*. The *manager(s)* should determine what arrangements are appropriate to meet the outcomes. Factors to be taken into account will include the size and complexity of the business; the number, experience and qualifications of the *employees*; the number of offices; and the nature of the work undertaken.

Where you are using a third party to provide services that you could provide, (often described as "outsourcing"), this chapter sets out the outcomes you need to achieve.

The outcomes in this chapter show how the *Principles* apply in the context of the management of your business.

Outcomes

You must achieve these outcomes:

O(7.1) you have a clear and effective governance structure and reporting lines;

O(7.2) you have effective systems and controls in place to achieve and comply with all the *Principles*, rules and outcomes and other requirements of the Handbook, where applicable;

O(7.3) you identify, monitor and manage risks to compliance with all the *Principles*, rules and outcomes and other requirements of the Handbook, if applicable to you, and take steps to address issues identified;

O(7.4) you maintain systems and controls for monitoring the financial stability of your *firm* and risks to money and *assets* entrusted to you by *clients* and others, and you take steps to address issues identified;

O(7.5) you comply with legislation applicable to your business, including anti-money laundering and data protection legislation;

O(7.6) you train individuals working in the *firm* to maintain a level of competence appropriate to their work and level of responsibility;

O(7.7) you comply with the statutory requirements for the direction and supervision of *reserved legal activities* and *immigration work*;

O(7.8) you have a system for supervising *clients'* matters, to include the regular checking of the quality of work by suitably competent and experienced people;

O(7.9) you do not outsource *reserved legal activities* to a *person* who is not authorised to conduct such activities;

O(7.10) subject to Outcome 7.9, where you outsource *legal activities* or any operational functions that are critical to the delivery of any *legal activities*, you ensure such outsourcing:

(a) does not adversely affect your ability to comply with, or the *SRA's* ability to monitor your compliance with, your obligations in the Handbook;

(b) is subject to contractual arrangements that enable the *SRA* or its agent to obtain information from, inspect the records (including electronic records) of, or enter the premises of, the third party, in relation to the outsourced activities or functions;

(c) does not alter your obligations towards your *clients*; and

(d) does not cause you to breach the conditions with which you must comply in order to be authorised and to remain so;

O(7.11) you identify, monitor and manage the compliance of your *overseas practices* with the SRA Overseas Rules;

O(7.12) you identify, monitor and manage all risks to your business which may arise from your *connected practices*;

O(7.13) you assess and purchase the level of professional indemnity insurance cover that is appropriate for your current and past practice, taking into account potential levels of claim by your *clients* and others and any alternative arrangements you or your *client* may make.

Indicative behaviours

Acting in the following way(s) may tend to show that you have achieved these outcomes and therefore complied with the *Principles*:

IB(7.1) safekeeping of documents and *assets* entrusted to the *firm*;

IB(7.2) controlling budgets, expenditure and cash flow;

IB(7.3) identifying and monitoring financial, operational and business continuity risks including *complaints*, credit risks and exposure, claims under legislation relating to matters such as data protection, IT failures and abuses, and damage to offices;

IB(7.4) making arrangements for the continuation of your *firm* in the event of absences and emergencies, for example holiday or sick leave, with the minimum interruption to *clients'* business;

IB(7.5) you maintain systems and controls for managing the risks posed by any financial inter-dependence which exists with your *connected practices*;

IB(7.6) you take appropriate action to control the use of your brand by any body or individual outside of England and Wales which is not an *overseas practice*.

In-house practice

Outcomes 7.5 and 7.7 apply to your *in-house practice*.

Outcomes 7.1 to 7.3, and 7.6 and 7.8 to 7.10 apply to you if you have management responsibilities.

Notes

(i) All of the chapters in the Code will be relevant to the management of your business, in particular those which require you to have systems and controls in place.

(ii) This chapter should also be read with the *SRA Authorisation Rules*, the SRA Financial Services (Conduct of Business) Rules 2001 and the *SRA Indemnity Insurance Rules*.

3RD SECTION: YOU AND YOUR REGULATOR

Chapter 10: You and your regulator

This chapter is about co-operation with your regulators and ombudsmen, primarily the *SRA* and the *Legal Ombudsman*.

The information which we request from you will help us understand any risks to *clients*, and the public interest more generally.

The outcomes in this chapter show how the *Principles* apply in the context of you and your regulator.

Outcomes

You must achieve these outcomes:

O(10.1) you ensure that you comply with all the reporting and notification requirements in the Handbook that apply to you;

O(10.2) you provide the *SRA* with information to enable the *SRA* to decide upon any application you make, such as for a practising certificate, registration, recognition or a licence and whether any conditions should apply;

O(10.3) you notify the *SRA* promptly of any material changes to relevant information about you including serious financial difficulty, action taken against you by another regulator and serious failure to comply with or achieve the *Principles*, rules, outcomes and other requirements of the Handbook;

O(10.4) you report to the *SRA* promptly, serious misconduct by any person or *firm* authorised by the *SRA*, or any *employee*, *manager* or *owner* of any such *firm* (taking into account, where necessary, your duty of confidentiality to your *client*);

O(10.5) you ensure that the *SRA* is in a position to assess whether any persons requiring prior approval are fit and proper at the point of approval and remain so;

O(10.6) you co-operate fully with the *SRA* and the *Legal Ombudsman* at all times including in relation to any investigation about a *claim for redress* against you;

O(10.7) you do not attempt to prevent anyone from providing information to the *SRA* or the *Legal Ombudsman*;

O(10.8) you comply promptly with any written notice from the *SRA*;

O(10.9) pursuant to a notice under Outcome 10.8, you:

(a) produce for inspection by the *SRA* *documents* held by you, or held under your control;

(b) provide all information and explanations requested; and

(c) comply with all requests from the *SRA* as to the form in which you produce any *documents* you hold electronically, and for photocopies of any *documents* to take away;

in connection with your *practice* or in connection with any trust of which you are, or formerly were, a trustee;

O(10.10) you provide any necessary permissions for information to be given, so as to enable the *SRA* to:

(a) prepare a report on any *documents* produced; and

(b) seek verification from *clients*, staff and the banks, building societies or other financial institutions used by you;

O(10.11) when required by the *SRA* in relation to a matter specified by the *SRA*, you:

(a) act promptly to investigate whether any *person* may have a *claim for redress* against you;

(b) provide the *SRA* with a report on the outcome of such an investigation, identifying *persons* who may have such a claim;

(c) notify *persons* that they may have a right of redress against you, providing them with information as to the nature of the possible claim, about the *firm's complaints* procedure and about the *Legal Ombudsman*; and

(d) ensure, where you have identified a *person* who may have a *claim for redress*, that the matter is dealt with under the *firm's complaints* procedure as if that *person* had made a *complaint*;

O(10.12) you do not attempt to abrogate to any third party your regulatory responsibilities in the Handbook, including the role of Compliance Officer for Legal Practice (*COLP*) or Compliance Officer for Finance and Administration (*COFA*);

O(10.13) once you are aware that your *firm* will cease to *practise*, you effect the orderly and transparent wind-down of activities, including informing the *SRA* before the *firm* closes.

Indicative behaviours

Acting in the following way(s) may tend to show that you have achieved these outcomes and therefore complied with the *Principles*:

IB(10.1) actively monitoring your achievement of the outcomes in order to improve standards and identify non-achievement of the outcomes;

IB(10.2) actively monitoring your financial stability and viability in order to identify and mitigate any risks to the public;

IB(10.3) notifying the *SRA* promptly of any indicators of serious financial difficulty, such as inability to pay your professional indemnity insurance premium, or rent or salaries, or breach of bank covenants;

IB(10.4) notifying the *SRA* promptly when you become aware that your business may not be financially viable to continue trading as a going concern, for example because of difficult trading conditions, poor cash flow, increasing overheads, loss of *managers* or *employees* and/or loss of sources of revenue;

IB(10.5) notifying the *SRA* of any serious issues identified as a result of monitoring referred to in IB10.1 and IB10.2 above, and producing a plan for remedying issues that have been identified;

IB(10.6) responding appropriately to any serious issues identified concerning competence and fitness and propriety of your *employees*, *managers* and *owners*;

IB(10.7) reporting disciplinary action taken against you by another regulator;

IB(10.8) informing the *SRA* promptly when you become aware of a significant change to your *firm*, for example:

(a) key personnel, such as a *manager*, *COLP* or *COFA*, joining or leaving the *firm*;

(b) a merger with, or an acquisition by or of, another *firm*;

IB(10.9) having appropriate arrangements for the orderly transfer of *clients'* property to another *authorised body* if your *firm* closes;

IB(10.10) having a "whistle-blowing" policy.

Acting in the following way(s) may tend to show that you have not achieved these outcomes and therefore not complied with the *Principles*:

IB(10.11) entering into an agreement which would attempt to preclude the *SRA* or the *Legal Ombudsman* from investigating any actual or potential *complaint* or allegation of professional misconduct;

IB(10.12) unless you can properly allege malice, issuing defamation proceedings in respect of a *complaint* to the *SRA*.

In-house practice

The outcomes in this chapter apply to your *in-house practice*.

Notes

(i) A notice under this chapter is deemed to be duly served:

(a) on the date on which it is delivered to or left at your last notified *practising* address;

(b) on the date on which it is sent electronically to your e-mail or fax address; or

(c) seven days after it has been sent by post or document exchange to your last notified *practising* address.

(ii) The outcomes in this chapter should be considered in conjunction with the following:

(a) Chapter 7 (Management of your business) – requirements for risk management procedures; and

(b) note (xv) to Rule 8 of the *SRA Authorisation Rules*.

[2.3] SRA Overseas Rules 2013[1]

[Last updated 1 October 2013]

Rules dated 30 August 2013 made by the Solicitors Regulation Authority Board under sections 31, 32, 33A, 34, 79 and 80 of the Solicitors Act 1974, sections 9 and 9A of the Administration of Justice Act 1985 and section 83 of, and paragraph 20 of schedule 11 to the Legal Services Act 2007, with the approval of the Legal Services Board under paragraph 19 of Schedule 4 to the Legal Services Act 2007 regulating the conduct of solicitors and their employees, registered European lawyers and their employees, registered foreign lawyers, recognised bodies and their managers and employees and licensed bodies and their managers and employees.

PART 1: THE OVERSEAS PRINCIPLES

Rule 1: Overseas Principles

1.1 You

(a) as a *regulated individual practising overseas* must ensure that you; or

(b) as a *responsible authorised body* must ensure that your *overseas practice*, and individual *managers*, and *members* and *owners* of your *overseas practice* (who are, for the purposes of these rules, 'those for whom you are responsible');

comply with the Overseas Principles stated below.

1.2 Each of the Overseas Principles stated below, is supplemented by a note to assist individuals and bodies to determine how best to comply with each Principle. These notes do not form part of the Principles and are for guidance only.

1.3 Overseas Principle 1: You must uphold the rule of the law and the proper administration of justice in England and Wales.

1. Since publication of version 15 of the SRA Handbook on 1 November 2015, the accounts rules for overseas practice have been set out in Part 3 of the SRA Overseas Rules 2013. (The accounts provisions applying to the practice of a registered European lawyer from an office in England and Wales of an exempt European practice remain in Part 7 of the SRA Accounts Rules 2011.)

The SRA Overseas Rules 2013 do not require firms to obtain or deliver an accountant's report (including a final report), unless required to do so by the SRA.

Transitional arrangements mean that firms with an accounting period end date before 1 November 2015 comply with rule 2C.1 of the SRA Overseas Rules 2013 in all dealings with client money (overseas), but follow the requirements for accountants' reports in version 14 of the SRA Accounts Rules 2011 (see **www.sra.org.uk**). These firms must therefore obtain and deliver the form of report for overseas practice (AR2), including a final report if appropriate. See also the annex at **6.4** on accountants' reports for overseas practice.

Guidance note

(i) Your obligations to *clients*, the *court* and third parties in England and Wales with whom you are dealing on behalf of your *clients* are unaffected by the location outside England and Wales from which you practise or by the location of your *overseas practice*.

1.4 Overseas Principle 2: You must act with integrity.

Guidance note

(i) Personal integrity is central to your role as the *client's* trusted adviser and should characterise all of your professional dealings with *clients*, the *court*, other *lawyers* and the public, wherever they are being conducted. You should use your judgment when considering how best to maintain your integrity at all times and avoid any behaviour outside England and Wales which undermines your character and suitability to be an *authorised person*. A *responsible authorised body* should ensure that its *overseas practices* observe comparable standards.

1.5 Overseas Principle 3: You must not allow your independence or the independence of your *overseas practice* to be compromised.

Guidance note

(i) "Independence" means your own independence and that of your firm and your *overseas practice*, and not merely your ability to give independent advice to a *client*. You should avoid giving control of your *overseas practice* to a third party beyond any local legal or regulatory ownership requirements.

1.6 Overseas Principle 4: You must act in the best interests of each *client*.

Guidance note

(i) You should act in good faith and do your best for each of the *clients* for whom you are (or your *overseas practice* is) acting. In particular, you should follow the local legal or regulatory requirements of the jurisdiction in which you or your *overseas practice* are practising in relation to confidentiality and conflicts of interest. If no such requirements exist, you should be guided by what you consider to be the best interests of each *client* in the circumstances.

1.7 Overseas Principle 5: You must provide a proper standard of service to your *clients*/the *clients* of your *overseas practice*.

Guidance note

(i) You should provide a proper standard of client care and work. This includes exercising competence, skill and diligence and taking into account the individual needs and circumstances of each *client* as well as the particular requirements and circumstances of the jurisdiction in which you are working. If your *client* meets the definition of a complainant under Section 128(3) of the Legal Services Act 2007 or the Legal Services Act 2007 (Legal Complaints) (Parties) Order 2010, you should inform the *client* who is regulating the legal services you or your *overseas practice* is providing to the *client*, what client protections are in place and whether they have the benefit of professional indemnity insurance or other indemnity.

1.8 Overseas Principle 6: You must not do anything which will or will be likely to bring into disrepute the *overseas practice*, yourself as a *regulated individual* or *responsible authorised body* or, by association, the legal profession in and of England and Wales.

Guidance note

(i) This includes any behaviour which occurs within or outside your professional *practice* which undermines your own reputation, that of the *practice* within which you are a *manager* or solicitor employee, or the wider reputation of the legal profession in and of England and Wales.

1.9 Overseas Principle 7: You must comply with your legal and regulatory obligations in England and Wales, and deal with your regulators and ombudsmen in England and Wales in an open, timely and co-operative manner and assist and not impede any *authorised person* or *authorised body* practising in England and Wales in complying with their legal and regulatory obligations and dealings with their regulators and ombudsmen.

Guidance note

(i) As a *responsible authorised body*, you should ensure that you, and those for whom you are responsible, comply with all of the reporting and notification requirements that apply to you and respond promptly and substantively to communications. You should ensure that you (and those for whom you are responsible) do not cause, contribute or facilitate a failure to comply with the *SRA's* regulatory arrangements by any *authorised person* or *authorised body* practising in England and Wales. *Regulated individuals practising overseas* should assist their *responsible authorised body* to comply with its regulatory obligations to the *SRA*.

1.10 Overseas Principle 8: You must run your business/the business of your *overseas practice* or carry out your/their role in the business effectively and in accordance with proper governance and sound financial and risk management principles.

Guidance note

(i) As a *responsible authorised body* you are required to ensure that your relations with your *overseas practice* accord with sound governance, financial and risk management principles. You should ensure that those for whom you are responsible under these rules assist you in meeting your obligations to the *SRA* in relation to managing any risks that your *overseas practice* might pose to your operations.

1.11 Overseas Principle 9: You must run your business/the business of your *overseas practice* or carry out your/their role in the business in a way that encourages equality of opportunity and respect for diversity.

Guidance note

(i) Every jurisdiction has its own legal, regulatory and cultural framework for equality and diversity. The *SRA* does not expect, or require, *regulated individuals* or bodies *practising overseas* to approach these issues as they would in England and Wales. It does, however, expect that *SRA regulated individuals* and bodies will do what they reasonably can to encourage equality of opportunity and respect for diversity, within the legal, regulatory and cultural context in which they are *practising overseas*.

1.12 Overseas Principle 10: You must protect *client* money and assets.

Guidance note

(i) In addition to complying with the specific requirements in the following parts of these rules, you and those for whom you are responsible should comply with local regulatory requirements in relation to *client* money, documents and assets and, in any event, you should ensure that they are protected appropriately.

PART 2: APPLICATION

Rule 2: Application

2.1 With regard to the Overseas Principles set out in Rule 1:

(a) they apply to you if you are a *regulated individual practising overseas*, or a *responsible authorised body* in relation to each of its *overseas practices*;

(b) you will be committing a breach if you permit another person to do anything on your behalf which, if done by you, would constitute a breach of these rules;

(c) you should ensure that you and those for whom you are responsible under these rules comply with all legal and regulatory obligations applicable in the jurisdiction outside England and Wales in which you or they are practising. You, and those for whom you are responsible under these rules, should not cause, contribute to or facilitate a failure to comply with those legal or regulatory obligations by any other person or body subject to them;

(d) where there is a conflict between compliance with the Overseas Principles set out in Rule 1 and/or the Overseas Accounts Rules or the Reporting Requirements set out in the following rules on the one hand, and any requirements placed upon you or those for whom you are responsible under these rules by local law or regulation on the other hand, the latter shall prevail, with the exception of Overseas Principle 6, which must be observed at all times;

(e) *Reserved legal activities* may only be conducted overseas from an *authorised body*. However, *regulated individuals* may conduct *reserved legal activities* overseas in the following circumstances:

(i) on an occasional basis from an *Overseas Practice* for clients in England and Wales provided that they comply with the *SRA Principles* and the provisions in Chapter 13A.3 to 13A.6 of the *SRA Code of Conduct* when conducting those *reserved legal activities*.

(ii) from an *Overseas Practice* under the Overseas Principles provided that this work is undertaken for clients based outside England and Wales.

(f) Notwithstanding (e) above, if you are a *solicitor* or a *REL*, and your *practice* predominantly and consistently comprises the provision of legal services to clients, or in relation to assets located in England and Wales, then regardless of where you are *established*, the *SRA Principles* and Chapter 13A of the *SRA Code of Conduct* will apply;

(g) if you are a *regulated individual practising overseas*, or a *responsible authorised body*, you must ensure that you, or those for whom you are responsible under these rules, comply with any requirements under:

(i) the SRA Property Selling Rules 2011;

(ii) the *SRA Insolvency Practice Rules*;

(iii) the *SRA European Cross-border Practice Rules*;

(iv) the *SRA Financial Services (Scope) Rules*;

(v) the SRA Financial Services (Conduct of Business) Rules 2001; and

(vi) the SRA Quality Assurance Scheme for Advocates (Crime) Regulations 2013;

which apply to you or your *overseas practice*.

PART 3: OVERSEAS ACCOUNTS RULES

Rule 2A: Purpose of the overseas accounts provisions

2A.1 The purpose of Part 3 of these rules is to describe how Overseas Principle 10 applies to *client money (overseas)* in order to ensure that it is protected and used for appropriate and proper purposes only.

Rule 2B: Application and waivers

2B.1 You:

(a) as a *regulated individual practising overseas* must ensure that you; or

(b) as a *responsible authorised body*, must ensure that your *overseas practice*, and those for whom you are responsible,

comply both with Parts 3 and 4 of these rules, and any applicable legal or regulatory requirements of the jurisdiction in which you or your *overseas practice* are practising relating to handling of client money or assets. If compliance with any provision of these rules would result in you or your *overseas practice* breaching local law or regulation, you may disregard that provision to the extent necessary to comply with the local requirements subject to the overriding obligations of Overseas Principle 6.

2B.2 In any particular case or cases the *SRA* may waive in writing any of the provisions of Parts 3 or 4 of these Rules, may place conditions on, and may revoke any waiver.

Rule 2C: Dealings with client money

2C.1 In all dealings with *client money (overseas)*, you as a *responsible authorised body* must ensure that your *overseas practice*:

(a) keeps *client money (overseas)*, separate from money which is not *client money (overseas)*;

(b) on receipt, pays *client money (overseas)* into a *client account (overseas)* without undue delay and keeps it there, unless the *client* has agreed otherwise or it is paid directly to a third party in the execution of a *trust* under which it is held;

(c) ensures by use of proper accounting systems and processes that *client money (overseas)* is used for the relevant *client's* matters only and for the purposes for which they have been paid;

(d) uses money held as *trustee* of a *trust* for the purposes of that *trust* only;

(e) establishes and maintains proper accounting systems and proper internal controls over those systems to ensure compliance with these rules;

(f) returns *client money (overseas)* to the person on whose behalf the money is held promptly, as soon as there is no longer any proper reason to retain those funds;

(g) keeps accounting records to show accurately the position with regard to the money held for each *client* and *trust* for a minimum period of six years; and

(h) accounts for interest on *client money (overseas)* in accordance with local law and customs of the jurisdiction in which you or your *overseas practice* are practising and otherwise when it is fair and reasonable to do so in all circumstances.

PART 4: REPORTING REQUIREMENTS

Rule 3: Reporting requirements

3.1 The *SRA* does not expect or require the same level of detailed monitoring, reporting and notification from those *practising overseas* as it would expect of *authorised persons* and *authorised bodies* in England and Wales. The level of reporting the *SRA* expects is proportionate to the level of regulatory risk posed by an *overseas practice*.

3.2 You, as a *regulated individual practising overseas* or as a *responsible authorised body*, must monitor any material or systemic breaches of the Overseas Principles that apply to you or to those for whom you are responsible and report them to the *SRA* when they occur, or as soon as reasonably practicable thereafter. In relation to an *overseas practice*, a material or systemic breach will relate either to the character and suitability of an individual, the financial vulnerability of an *overseas practice* outside of established business planning, or a pattern of behaviour within an *overseas practice* that infringes Overseas Principle 6. Notifications by the compliance officer of a *responsible authorised body*, or by another person on behalf of an *overseas practice* will satisfy these requirements without separate notifications from each individual or body who has knowledge of the breach. For example, you will be required to:

(a) notify the *SRA*, if you, or any of the *partners*, *members*, *managers*, solicitor employees or other professionally qualified employees in your *overseas practice*, are convicted by any *court* of a criminal offence or become subject to disciplinary action by another regulator;

(b) notify the *SRA* immediately if you believe that your firm or your *overseas practice* is in serious financial difficulty;

(c) provide the *SRA* with documents held by you or your *overseas practice*, to which it is entitled, and any necessary permissions to access information as soon as possible following a notice from the *SRA* to do so;

(d) provide the *SRA*, if you are a *responsible authorised body*, with an annual return which:

 (i) identifies the contact details of the office(s) from which you are, or your *overseas practice* is, practising, and

 (ii) confirms that you have fulfilled your reporting and notification obligations.

3.3 The *SRA* may require the delivery of an accountant's report by you as a *responsible authorised body* in respect of your *overseas practice*(s).

3.4 This report must:

(a) be signed by a qualified accountant approved by the *SRA*;

(b) contain the information specifically requested by the *SRA* in relation to the protection and movement of *client money (overseas)*;

(c) contain a description of the reporting accountant's examination of your records and relevant documentation;

(d) contain a statement from the reporting accountant which confirms that, save for trivial breaches:

 (i) you have complied with rule 2C; or

 (ii) where you have breached the requirements of rule 2C this is because you have been bound by local law or regulation to do so, giving details of all such breaches.

3.5 You as a *regulated individual practising overseas* or a *responsible authorised body* must promptly comply with a written notice from the *SRA* that you must produce for inspection by the appointee of the *SRA* all documents held by you or held under your control and all information and explanations requested.

[3] Glossary

[3.1] SRA Handbook Glossary 2012 (extracts)

[Last updated 12 August 2016]

PART 1: INTRODUCTION AND PREAMBLE

Introduction

This section of the Handbook contains the SRA Handbook Glossary.

The SRA Handbook Glossary comprises a set of defined terms which are used in the SRA Handbook. Terms being used in their defined sense appear as italicised text within the individual sets of provisions of the SRA Handbook. The same terms in the SRA Handbook may appear as italicised text in some cases but not in others. Where they are not italicised, for reasons relating to the specific context, they are not being used in their defined sense and take their natural meaning in that context.

The Glossary also contains interpretation and transitional provisions.

Preamble

The SRA Handbook Glossary dated 18 April 2012 made by the Solicitors Regulation Authority Board.

Made under Part I, Part II, section 79 and 80 of, and paragraph 6B of Schedule 1 to, the Solicitors Act 1974; and section 9 and 9A of, and paragraphs 14A, 14B and 32 to 34 of Schedule 2 to, the Administration of Justice Act 1985; and section 83 of, and Schedule 11 to and paragraph 6 of Schedule 14 to, the Legal Services Act 2007; and paragraphs 2 and 3 of Schedule 14 to the Courts and Legal Services Act 1990.

Subject to the approval of the Legal Services Board under paragraph 19 of Schedule 4 to the Legal Services Act 2007 and coming into force on the day it is approved.

PART 2: GENERAL

Rule 1: Application

1.1 Subject to Rule 1.2 below:

(a) the definitions set out at Rule 2 below shall apply to the corresponding term where this appears in italics in the *SRA Handbook*; and

(b) the interpretation provisions set out at Rule 3 below shall apply to the *SRA Handbook*.

1.2 This Rule shall not apply to the SRA Indemnity Insurance Rules 2011, the SRA Indemnity (Enactment) Rules 2011 and the SRA Indemnity Rules 2011 until 1 October 2012.

Rule 2: Definitions [extracts]

accounting period has the meaning given in Rule 33 of the *SRA Accounts Rules*.

agreed fee has the meaning given in Rule 17.5 of the *SRA Accounts Rules*.

AJA means the Administration of Justice Act 1985.

approved regulator means any body listed as an approved regulator in paragraph 1 of Schedule 4 to the *LSA* or designated as an approved regulator by an order under paragraph 17 of that Schedule.

assets includes money, documents, wills, deeds, investments and other property.

authorised body means:

(i) a body that has been authorised by the *SRA* to practise as a *licensed body* or a *recognised body*; or

(ii) a *sole practitioner's practice* that has been authorised by the *SRA* as a *recognised sole practice*.

authorised non-SRA firm means a firm which is authorised to carry on *legal activities* by an *approved regulator* other than the *SRA*.

authorised person

(i) subject to sub-paragraph (ii) below, means a *person* who is authorised by the *SRA* or another *approved regulator* to carry on a *legal activity* and for the purposes of the *SRA Authorisation Rules* and the *SRA Practice Framework Rules* includes a *solicitor*, a *sole practitioner*, an *REL*, an *EEL*, an *RFL*, an *authorised body*, an *authorised non-SRA firm* and a *European corporate practice* and the terms "*authorised individual*" and "non-authorised person" shall be construed accordingly; and

(ii) in the *SRA Financial Services (Scope) Rules*, has the meaning given in section 31 of *FSMA*.

bank has the meaning given in section 87(1) of the *SA*.

BSB means the Bar Standards Board.

building society means a building society within the meaning of the Building Societies Act 1986.

claim means a demand for, or an assertion of a right to, civil compensation or civil damages or an intimation of an intention to seek such compensation or damages. For these purposes, an obligation on an *insured firm* and/or any *insured* to remedy a breach of the Solicitors' Accounts Rules 1998 (as amended from time to time), or any rules (including, without limitation, the *SRA Accounts Rules*) which replace the Solicitors' Accounts Rules 1998 in whole or in part, shall be treated as a claim, and the obligation to remedy such breach shall be treated as a civil liability for the purposes of clause 1 of the *MTC*, whether or not any *person* makes a demand for, or an assertion of a right to, civil compensation or civil damages or an intimation of an intention to seek such compensation or damages as a result of such breach, except where any such obligation may arise as a result of the insolvency of a bank (as defined in section 87 of the *SA*) or a *building society* which holds client money in a client account of the *insured firm* or the failure of such bank or *building society* generally to repay monies on demand.

claim for redress has the meaning given in section 158 of the *LSA*.

client means:

(i) the *person* for whom you act and, where the context permits, includes prospective and former clients;

(ii) in Parts 1–6 of the *SRA Accounts Rules*, the person for whom *you* act; and

(iii) in the *SRA Financial Services (Scope) Rules*, in relation to any *regulated activities* carried on by a *firm* for a trust or the estate of a deceased person (including a controlled trust), the trustees or personal representatives in their capacity as such and not any *person* who is a beneficiary under the trust or interested in the estate.

client account has the meaning given in Rule 13.2 of the *SRA Accounts Rules*.

client account (overseas) means an account at a bank or similar institution, subject to supervision by a public authority, which is used only for the purpose of holding *client money (overseas)*, and the title, designation or account details allow the account to be identified as belonging to the client or clients of a *solicitor* or *REL* or that they are being held subject to a *trust*.

client money has the meaning given in Rule 12 of the *SRA Accounts Rules*.

client money (overseas) means money held or received for a *client* in respect of legal services that you are providing or as *trustee*, and all other money which is not *office money (overseas)*. This includes money held or received:

(i) as *trustee*;

(ii) as agent, bailee, stakeholder, or as the donee of a power of attorney, or as a liquidator, trustee in bankruptcy, *Court of Protection deputy* or trustee of an occupational pension scheme;

(iii) for payment of unpaid *professional disbursements*;

(iv) for payment of taxes, duties or fees on behalf of clients or third parties;

(v) as a payment on account of *costs* and *disbursements* generally;

(vi) jointly with another person outside of your practice;

(vii) to the sender's order.

COFA means a compliance officer for finance and administration in accordance with Rule 8.5 of the *SRA Authorisation Rules*, or Regulation 4.8 of the *SRA Practising Regulations*, and in relation to a *licensable body* is a reference to its *HOFA*.

COLP means compliance officer for legal practice in accordance with Rule 8.5 of the *SRA Authorisation Rules* or Regulation 4.8 of the *SRA Practising Regulations*, and in relation to a *licensable body* is a reference to its *HOLP*.

Companies Acts means the Companies Act 1985 and the Companies Act 2006.

company means a company incorporated in an *Establishment Directive state* and registered under the *Companies Acts* or a *societas Europaea*.

complaint means an oral or written expression of dissatisfaction which alleges that the complainant has suffered (or may suffer) financial loss, distress, inconvenience or other detriment.

connected practice means a body providing legal services, established outside England and Wales which is not an overseas practice or an excluded body but is otherwise connected to an authorised body in England and Wales, by virtue of:

(i) being a parent undertaking, within the meaning of section 1162 of the Companies Act 2006, of the authorised body;

(ii) being jointly managed or owned, or having a partner, member or owner in common, or controlled by or, with the authorised body;

(iii) participating in a joint enterprise or across its practice generally, sharing costs, revenue or profits related to the provision of legal services with the authorised body; or

(iv) common branding;

and in this definition:

(A) a "body" means a natural person or company, limited liability partnership or partnership or other body corporate or unincorporated association or business entity; and

(B) an "excluded body" means a body which is part of:

(I) a Verein or similar group structure involving more than one body providing legal services in respect of which the authorised body in England and Wales connected to it is not regarded as being the body which is the headquarters of that Verein or similar group structure or a significant part of it; or

(II) a joint practice, alliance or association or association with the authorised body in England and Wales connected to it which is controlled by a body providing legal services outside of England and Wales; or

(III) a group of affiliated bodies providing legal services which is not managed or controlled by an authorised body in England and Wales.

(C) A "joint enterprise" means any contractual arrangements between two or more independent bodies which provide legal services, for profit and/or other defined purpose or goal which apply generally between them, not just agreed on a matter by matter basis.

(D) "Common branding" means the use of a name, term, design, symbol, words or a combination of these that identifies two or more legal practices as distinct from other legal practices or an express statement that a legal practice is practising in association with one or more other named firms.

costs means *your fees* and *disbursements*.

Court of Protection deputy

(i) for the purposes of the *SRA Accounts Rules* includes a deputy who was appointed by the Court of Protection as a receiver under the Mental Health Act 1983 before the commencement date of the Mental Capacity Act 2005; and

(ii) for the purposes of the *SRA Authorisation Rules* also includes equivalents in other *Establishment Directive states*.

director means a director of a company; and in relation to a *societas Europaea* includes:

(i) in a two-tier system, a member of the management organ and a member of the supervisory organ; and

(ii) in a one-tier system, a member of the administrative organ.

disbursement means, in respect of those activities for which the practice is regulated by the *SRA*, any sum spent or to be spent on behalf of the *client* or trust (including any VAT element).

document in Chapter 10 of the *SRA Code of Conduct*, includes documents, whether written or electronic, relating to the *firm's client accounts* and *office accounts*.

employee means an individual who is:

(i) engaged under a contract of service by a *firm* or its wholly owned service company;

(ii) engaged under a contract for services, made between a *firm* or organisation and:

(A) that individual;

(B) an employment agency; or

(C) a *company* which is not held out to the public as providing legal services and is wholly owned and directed by that individual; or

(iii) a *solicitor*, *REL* or *RFL* engaged under a contract of service or a contract for services by an *authorised non-SRA firm*;

(iv) a *solicitor*, *REL* or *RFL* engaged under a contract of service or a contract for services by a person, business or organisation,

under which the *firm*, *authorised non-SRA firm*, person, business, or organisation has exclusive control over the individual's time for all or part of the individual's working week; or in relation to which the *firm* or organisation has designated the individual as a fee earner in accordance with arrangements between the *firm* or organisation and the Lord Chancellor (or any body established by the Lord Chancellor to provide or facilitate the provision of services) pursuant to the provisions of the Legal Aid, Sentencing and Punishment of Offenders Act 2012, save that:

(A) for the purposes of the *SRA Financial Services (Scope) Rules*, means an individual who is employed in connection with the *firm's regulated activities* under a contract of service or under a contract for services such that he or she is held out as an employee or consultant of the *firm*; and

(B) for the purposes of the *SRA Indemnity Insurance Rules*, means any person other than a *principal*:

(I) employed or otherwise engaged in the *insured firm's practice* (including under a contract for services) including, without limitation, as a *solicitor*, lawyer, *trainee solicitor* or trainee lawyer, consultant, associate, locum tenens, agent, *appointed person*, office or clerical staff member or otherwise;

(II) seconded to work in the *insured firm's practice*; or

(III) seconded by the *insured firm* to work elsewhere;

but does not include any person who is engaged by the *insured firm* under a contract for services in respect of any work where that person is required, whether under the *SRA Indemnity Insurance Rules* or under the rules of any other professional body, to take out or to be insured under separate professional indemnity insurance in respect of that work.

Establishment Directive means the Establishment of Lawyers Directive 98/5/EC.

Establishment Directive profession means any profession listed in Article 1.2(a) of the *Establishment Directive*, including a solicitor, barrister or advocate of the *UK*.

Establishment Directive state means a state to which the *Establishment Directive* applies.

Exempt European Practice means:

(i) a *lawyer's* practice formed in an *Establishment Directive state* which is regulated as such in that state and which is a structure in which *lawyers* are permitted to practise in that state; and

(ii) whose ultimate beneficial owners do not include any *practising lawyers of England and Wales*; and

(iii) whose main place of business is situated and carried on in an *Establishment Directive state* other than the United Kingdom; and

(iv) which does not carry on any *reserved legal activity*.

fees means *your* own charges or profit costs (including any VAT element).

firm means:

(i) save as provided in paragraphs (ii) and (iii) below, an *authorised body* or a body or *person* which should be authorised by the *SRA* as a *recognised body* or whose practice should be authorised as a *recognised sole practice* (but which could not be authorised by another *approved regulator*); and for the purposes of the *SRA Code of Conduct* and the *SRA Accounts Rules* can also include in-house practice;

(ii) in the *SRA Indemnity Insurance Rules*:

(A) any *recognised body* (as constituted from time to time); or

(B) any *solicitor* or *REL* who is a *sole practitioner*, unless that *sole practitioner* is a *non-SRA firm*; or

(C) any *partnership* (as constituted from time to time) which is eligible to become a *recognised body* and which meets the requirements applicable to *recognised bodies* set out in the *SRA Practice Framework Rules* and the *SRA Authorisation Rules*, unless that *partnership* is a *non-SRA firm* or an *Exempt European Practice*; or

(D) any *licensed body* in respect of its *regulated activities*;

whether before or during any relevant *indemnity period*;

(iii) in the *SRA European Cross-border Practice Rules*, means any business through which a *solicitor* or *REL* carries on *practice* other than *in-house practice*.

firm (overseas) means any business through which a *solicitor* or *REL* carries on practice other than in-house practice.

general client account has the meaning given in Rule 13.5(b) of the *SRA Accounts Rules*.

immigration work means the provision of immigration advice and immigration services, as defined in section 82 of the Immigration and Asylum Act 1999.

in-house practice means *practice* as a *solicitor*, *REL* or *RFL* (as appropriate) in accordance with Rules 1.1(c)(ii), 1.1(d)(ii), 1.1(e), 1.2(f), 2.1(c)(ii), 2.1(d)(ii), 2.1(e), 2.2(f), 3.1(b)(ii) or 3.1(c)(ii) of the *SRA Practice Framework Rules* and "in-house" shall be construed accordingly.

interest includes a sum in lieu of interest.

lawyer means a member of one of the following professions, entitled to practise as such:

(i) the profession of solicitor, barrister or advocate of the *UK*;

(ii) a profession whose members are authorised to carry on *legal activities* by an *approved regulator* other than the *SRA*;

(iii) an *Establishment Directive profession* other than a *UK* profession;

(iv) a legal profession which has been approved by the *SRA* for the purpose of *recognised bodies* in England and Wales; and

(v) any other regulated legal profession specified by the *SRA* for the purpose of this definition.

lawyer-controlled body means:

(i) an *authorised body* in which *lawyers of England and Wales* constitute the national group of *lawyers* with the largest (or equal largest) share of control of the body either as individual *managers* or by their share in the control of bodies which are *managers*;

(ii) for the purposes of Part 7 (Overseas practice) of the *SRA Accounts Rules* the definition at sub-paragraph (i) above applies save that the second reference to "lawyers" is to be given its natural meaning and the references to *managers* are to be read as *managers (overseas)*.

lawyer of England and Wales means:

(i) a *solicitor*; or

(ii) an individual who is authorised to carry on *legal activities* in England and Wales by an *approved regulator* other than the *SRA*, but excludes a member of an *Establishment Directive profession* registered with the *BSB* under the *Establishment Directive*.

legal activity has the meaning given in section 12 of the *LSA*, and includes any *reserved legal activity* and any other activity which consists of the provision of legal advice or assistance, or representation in connection with the application of the law or resolution of legal disputes.

Legal Ombudsman means the scheme administered by the Office for Legal Complaints under Part 6 of the *LSA*.

licensable body means a body which meets the criteria in Rule 14 (Eligibility criteria and fundamental requirements for licensed bodies) of the *SRA Practice Framework Rules*.

licensed body means a body licensed by the *SRA* under Part 5 of the *LSA*.

licensing authority means an *approved regulator* which is designated as a licensing authority under Part 1 of Schedule 10 to the *LSA*, and whose licensing rules have been approved for the purposes of the *LSA*.

LLP means a limited liability partnership incorporated under the Limited Liability Partnerships Act 2000.

local authority means any of those bodies which are listed in section 270 of the Local Government Act 1972 or in section 21(1) of the Local Government and Housing Act 1989.

LSA means the Legal Services Act 2007.

manager means:

(i) a *member* of an *LLP*;

(ii) a *director* of a *company*;

(iii) a *partner* in a *partnership*; or

(iv) in relation to any other body, a member of its governing body.

manager (overseas) means:

(i) a member of an *LLP*;

(ii) a director of a company;

(iii) a *partner* in a *partnership*; or

(iv) in relation to any other body, a member of its governing body.

MDP means a *licensed body* which is a multi-disciplinary practice providing a range of different services, only some of which are regulated by the *SRA*.

mixed payment has the meaning given in Rule 18.1 of the *SRA Accounts Rules*.

non-lawyer means:

(i) an individual who is not a *lawyer* practising as such; or

(ii) a *body corporate* or *partnership* which is not:

(A) an *authorised body*;

(B) an *authorised non-SRA firm*; or

(C) a business, carrying on the practice of *lawyers* from an office or offices outside England and Wales, in which a controlling majority of the *owners* and *managers* are *lawyers*;

save in Part 7 (Overseas) of the *SRA Accounts Rules* where the term "lawyer" is to be given its natural meaning.

non-solicitor employer means any *employer* other than a *recognised body*, *recognised sole practice*, *licensed body* or *authorised non-SRA firm*.

office account means an account of the *firm* for holding *office money* and/or *out-of-scope money*, or other means of holding *office money* or *out-of-scope money* (for example, the office cash box or an account holding money regulated by a regulator other than the *SRA*).

office money has the meaning given in Rule 12 of the *SRA Accounts Rules*.

out-of-scope money means money held or received by an *MDP* in relation to activities that are not *regulated activities*.

overseas means outside England and Wales.

overseas practice

(i) means:

(A) a branch office of an *authorised body*;

(B) a *subsidiary company* of an *authorised body*;

(C) a subsidiary undertaking, within the meaning of section 1162 of the Companies Act 2006, of an *authorised body*;

(D) an entity whose business, management or ownership are otherwise in fact or law controlled by an *authorised body*;

(E) an individual acting as a representative (whether as an employee or agent) of an *authorised body*; or

(F) a sole principal whose business, management or ownership are otherwise in fact or law controlled by an *authorised body*,

established outside England and Wales and providing legal services; and

(ii) in the *SRA Indemnity Rules* means a *practice* carried on wholly from an *overseas* office or offices, including a *practice* deemed to be a *separate practice* by virtue of paragraph (ii) of the definition of *separate practice*.

owner means, in relation to a body, a *person* with any interest in the body, save that:

(i) in the *SRA Authorisation Rules*, the *SRA Practice Framework Rules* and the *SRA Practising Regulations* owner means any *person* who holds a *material interest* in an *authorised body*, and in the case of a *partnership*, any *partner* regardless of whether they hold a *material interest* in the *partnership*; and

(ii) for the purposes of the *SRA Principles* and the *SRA Code of Conduct* means a *person* who holds a *material interest* in the body; and

(iii) for the purposes of the *SRA Suitability Test* includes owners who have no active role in the running of the business as well as owners who do,

and "own" and "owned by" shall be construed accordingly.

partner means a *person* who is or is held out as a partner in a *partnership*.

partnership means a body that is not a *body corporate* in which *persons* are, or are held out as, *partners*, save that in the *MTC* means an unincorporated *insured firm* in which *persons* are or are held out as *partners* and does not include an *insured firm* incorporated as an *LLP*.

person includes a body of persons (corporate or unincorporated).

practice means the activities, in that capacity, of:

(i) a *solicitor*;

(ii) an *REL*, from an office or offices within the *UK*;

(iii) a member of an *Establishment Directive profession* registered with the *BSB* under the *Establishment Directive*, carried out from an office or offices in England and Wales;

(iv) an *RFL*, from an office or offices within England and Wales, as:

(A) an *employee* of a *recognised sole practice*; or

(B) a *manager*, *employee*, *member* or *interest holder* of an *authorised body* or a *manager*, *employee* or owner of an *authorised non-SRA firm*;

(v) an *authorised body*;

(vi) a *manager* of an *authorised body*;

(vii) a person employed in England and Wales by an *authorised body*;

(viii) a *lawyer of England and Wales*; or

(ix) an *authorised non-SRA firm*;

and "practise" and "practising" should be construed accordingly; save for in:

(i) the *SRA Indemnity Insurance Rules* where "practice" means the whole or such part of the *private practice* of a *firm* as is carried on from one or more offices in England and Wales;

(ii) the *SRA Indemnity Rules* where it means a practice to the extent that:

(A) in relation to a *licensed body*, it carries on *regulated activities*; and

(B) in all other cases, it carries on *private practice* providing professional services as a sole *solicitor* or *REL* or as a *partnership* of a type referred to in Rule 6.1(d) to 6.1(f) and consisting of or including one or more *solicitors* and/or *RELs*, and shall include the business or practice carried on by a *recognised body* in the providing of professional services such as are provided by individuals practising in *private practice* as *solicitors* and/or *RELs* or by such individuals in *partnership* with *RFLs*, whether such practice is carried on by the *recognised body* alone or in *partnership* with one or more *solicitors*, *RELs* and/or other *recognised bodies*; and

(iii) in the *SRA Overseas Rules* where it shall be given its natural meaning.

practice from an office includes *practice* carried on:

(i) from an office at which you are based; or

(ii) from an office of a *firm* in which you are the *sole practitioner*, or a *manager*, or in which you have an ownership interest, even if you are not based there,

save that for the purposes of Part 7 (Overseas) of the *SRA Accounts Rules* the term "practice" is to be given its natural meaning, and references to "firm" and "manager" are to be read as references to "*firm (overseas)*" and to "*manager (overseas)*";

and "practising from an office" and "practises from an office" should be construed accordingly.

practising overseas means the conduct of a practice:

(i) of an overseas practice;

(ii) of a manager, member or owner of an overseas practice in that capacity;

(iii) of a solicitor *established* outside England and Wales for the purpose of providing legal services in an overseas jurisdiction; and

(iv) of an REL *established* in Scotland or Northern Ireland for the purpose of providing legal services in those jurisdictions.

principal

(i) subject to paragraphs (ii) to (iv) means:

(A) a *sole practitioner*;

(B) a *partner* in a *partnership*;

(C) in the case of a *recognised body* which is an *LLP* or *company*, the *recognised body* itself;

(D) in the case of a *licensed body* which is an *LLP* or *company*, the *licensed body* itself;

(E) the principal *solicitor* or *REL* (or any one of them) employed by a *non-solicitor employer* (for example, in a law centre or in commerce and industry); or

(F) in relation to any other body, a member of its governing body;

(ii) in the *SRA Authorisation Rules*, *SRA Practice Framework Rules* and *SRA Practising Regulations*, means a *sole practitioner* or a *partner* in a *partnership*;

(iii) in the *SRA Indemnity Insurance Rules* means:

(A) where the *firm* is or was:

(I) a *sole practitioner* – that practitioner;

(II) a *partnership* – each *partner*;

(III) a *company* with a share capital – each *director* of that *company* and any *person* who:

(01) is held out as a *director*; or

(02) beneficially owns the whole or any part of a share in the *company*; or

(03) is the ultimate beneficial owner of the whole or any part of a share in the *company*;

(IV) a *company* without a share capital – each *director* of that *company* and any *person* who:

(01) is held out as a *director*; or

(02) is a *member* of the *company*; or

(03) is the ultimate owner of the whole or any part of a *body corporate* or other legal person which is a *member* of the *company*;

(V) an *LLP* – each *member* of that *LLP*, and any *person* who is the ultimate owner of the whole or any part of a *body corporate* or other legal person which is a *member* of the *LLP*;

(B) where a *body corporate* or other legal person is a *partner* in the *firm*, any *person* who is within paragraph (A)(III) of this definition (including sub-paragraphs (01) and (03) thereof), paragraph (A)(IV) of this definition (including sub-paragraphs (01) and (03) thereof), or paragraph (A)(V) of this definition;

(iv) in the *SRA Indemnity Rules*, means:

(A) a *solicitor* who is a *partner* or a sole *solicitor* within the meaning of section 87 of the *SA*, or an *REL* who is a *partner*, or who is a sole practitioner, or an *RFL* or *non-registered European lawyer* who is a *partner*, and includes any *solicitor*, *REL*, *RFL* or *non-registered European lawyer* held out as a principal; and

(B) additionally in relation to a *practice* carried on by a *recognised body* or a *licensed body* alone, or a *practice* in which a *recognised body* or a *licensed body* is or is held out to be a *partner*:

(I) a *solicitor*, *REL*, *RFL* or *non-registered European lawyer* (and in the case of a *licensed body* any other person) who:

(01) beneficially owns the whole or any part of a share in such *recognised body* or *licensed body* (in each case, where it is a *company* with a share capital); or

(02) is a member of such *recognised body* or *licensed body* (in each case, where it is a *company* without a share capital or an *LLP* or a *partnership* with legal personality); or

(II) a *solicitor*, *REL*, *RFL* or *non-registered European lawyer* (and in the case of a *licensed body* any other person) who is:

(01) the ultimate beneficial owner of the whole or any part of a share in such *recognised body* or *licensed body* (in each case, where the *recognised* body or *licensed body* is a *company* with a share capital); or

(02) the ultimate owner of a member or any part of a member of such *recognised body* or *licensed body* (in each case, where the *recognised body* or *licensed body* is a *company* without a share capital or an *LLP* or a *partnership* with legal personality).

private loan means a loan other than one provided by an institution which provides loans on standard terms in the normal course of its activities.

professional disbursement means, in respect of those activities for which the practice is regulated by the *SRA*, the fees of counsel or other *lawyer*, or of a professional or other agent or expert instructed by *you*, including the fees of interpreters, translators, process servers, surveyors and estate agents but not travel agents' charges.

recognised body means a body recognised by the *SRA* under section 9 of the *AJA*.

recognised sole practice means the *practice* of a sole *solicitor* or *REL* which is recognised by the *SRA* under section 9 of the *AJA*.

regular payment has the meaning given in Rule 19 of the *SRA Accounts Rules*.

regulated activity means:

(i) subject to sub-paragraph (ii) below:

(A) any *reserved legal activity*;

(B) any *non-reserved legal activity* except, in relation to an *MDP*, any such activity that is excluded on the terms of the licence;

(C) any other activity in respect of which a *licensed body* is regulated pursuant to Part 5 of the *LSA*; and

(ii) in the *SRA Financial Services (Scope) Rules*, an activity which is specified in the *Regulated Activities Order*.

regulated individual means:

(i) a solicitor;

(ii) an REL; and

(iii) a manager, member or owner of an *overseas practice*.

regulatory arrangements has the meaning given to it by section 21 of the *LSA*, and includes all rules and regulations of the *SRA* in relation to the authorisation, *practice*, conduct, discipline and qualification of persons carrying on *legal activities* and the accounts rules and indemnification and compensation arrangements in relation to their *practice*.

REL means registered European lawyer, namely, an individual registered with the *SRA* under regulation 17 of the European Communities (Lawyer's Practice) Regulations 2000 (SI 2000/ no.1119).

REL-controlled body means an *authorised body* in which *RELs*, or *RELs* together with *lawyers of England and Wales* and/or European lawyers registered with the *BSB*, constitute the national group of lawyers with the largest (or equal largest) share of control of the body, either as individual *managers (overseas)* or by their share in the control of bodies which are *managers (overseas)*, and for this purpose *RELs* and European lawyers registered with the *BSB* belong to the national group of England and Wales.

reserved legal activity has the meaning given in section 12 of the *LSA*, and includes the exercise of a right of audience, the conduct of litigation, reserved instrument activities, probate activities, notarial activities and the administration of oaths, as defined in Schedule 2 to the *LSA*.

responsible authorised body in respect of an *overseas practice* means the *authorised body* referred to in whichever of paragraph (i)(A) to (F) of the definition of "overseas practice" is applicable to that practice.

RFL means registered foreign lawyer, namely, an individual registered with the *SRA* under section 89 of the Courts and Legal Services Act 1990.

SA means the Solicitors Act 1974.

separate designated client account has the meaning given in Rule 13.5(a) of the *SRA Accounts Rules*.

societas Europaea means a European public limited liability company within the meaning of Article 1 of Council Regulation 2157/2001/EC.

Society means the Law Society, in accordance with section 87 of the *SA*.

sole practitioner means a *solicitor* or an *REL practising* as a sole principal in a *practice* (other than an incorporated *practice*) and does not include a *solicitor* or an *REL practising in-house*, save for the purposes of:

(i) the *SRA Accounts Rules* and *SRA Indemnity Insurance Rules* where references to "practising" are to be given their natural meaning; and

(ii) the *SRA Authorisation Rules* where it includes (as the context may require) a *solicitor* or *REL* intending to *practise* as a sole principal in a *practice* (other than incorporated *practice*).

solicitor means a person who has been admitted as a solicitor of the Senior Courts of England and Wales and whose name is on the roll kept by the *Society* under section 6 of the *SA*, save that in the *SRA Indemnity Insurance Rules* includes a person who *practises* as a solicitor whether or not he or she has in force a practising certificate, and also includes *practice* under home title of a former *REL* who has become a solicitor.

SRA means the Solicitors Regulation Authority, and reference to the SRA as an *approved regulator* or *licensing authority* means the SRA carrying out regulatory functions assigned to the *Society* as an *approved regulator* or *licensing authority*.

SRA Accounts Rules means the SRA Accounts Rules 2011.

SRA Authorisation Rules means the SRA Authorisation Rules 2011.

SRA Code of Conduct means the SRA Code of Conduct 2011.

SRA European Cross-border Practice Rules means the SRA European Cross-border Practice Rules 2011.

SRA Financial Services (Scope) Rules means the SRA Financial Services (Scope) Rules 2001.

SRA Handbook Glossary means the SRA Handbook Glossary 2012, and references to the "Glossary" shall be interpreted accordingly.

SRA Indemnity Rules means the SRA Indemnity Rules 2012.

SRA Practice Framework Rules means the SRA Practice Framework Rules 2011.

SRA Principles means the SRA Principles in the *SRA Handbook* and "Principles" shall be interpreted accordingly.

statutory undertakers means:

(i) any persons authorised by any enactment to carry on any railway, light railway, tramway, road transport, water transport, canal, inland navigation, dock, harbour, pier or lighthouse undertaking or any undertaking for the supply of hydraulic power; and

(ii) any licence holder within the meaning of the Electricity Act 1989, any public gas supplier, any water or sewerage undertaker, the Environment Agency, any public telecommunications operator, the Post Office, the Civil Aviation Authority and any relevant airport operator within the meaning of Part V of the Airports Act 1986.

temporary practice overseas means the situation where:

(i) a *solicitor* is practising but not established overseas; or

(ii) an *REL* is practising from an office in Scotland or Northern Ireland,

but the solicitor or REL is not *practising overseas*.

trustee includes a personal representative, and "trust" includes the duties of a personal representative.

UK means United Kingdom.

without delay means, in normal circumstances, either on the day of receipt or on the next working day.

you means:

(i) for the purposes of the *SRA Training Regulations* any person intending to be a *solicitor*, other than those seeking admission under the *QLTSR*;

(ii) for the purposes of the SRA Training Regulations 2011 Part 3 a *solicitor* or an *REL*;

(iii) for the purposes of the *SRA Admission Regulations* any person intending to be a *solicitor*;

(iv) for the purpose of the *QLTSR* a person seeking admission as a *solicitor* via transfer in accordance with those regulations;

(v) for the purpose of the *SRA Suitability Test* any individual intending to be a *solicitor*, and any person seeking authorisation as an *authorised role holder* under the *SRA Authorisation Rules*;

(vi) for the purposes of the *SRA Accounts Rules* (save for Part 7 (Overseas practice)):

(A) a *solicitor*; or

(B) an *REL*;

in either case who is:

(I) a *sole practitioner*;

(II) a *partner* in a *partnership* which is a *recognised body*, *licensed body* or *authorised non-SRA firm*, or in a *partnership* which should be a *recognised body* but has not been recognised by the *SRA*;

(III) an assistant, associate, professional support lawyer, consultant, locum or person otherwise employed in the practice of a *recognised body*, *licensed body*, *recognised sole practice* or *authorised non-SRA firm*; or of a *partnership* which should be a *recognised body* but has not been recognised by the *SRA*, or of a *sole practitioner* whose *practice* should be a *recognised sole practice* but has not been authorised by the *SRA*; and "employed" in this context shall be interpreted in accordance with the definition of "employee" for the purposes of the *SRA Code of Conduct*;

(IV) employed as an in-house lawyer by a *non-solicitor employer* (for example, in a law centre or in commerce and industry);

(V) a *director* of a *company* which is a *recognised body*, *licensed body* or *authorised non-SRA firm*, or of a *company* which is a *manager* of a *recognised body*, *licensed body* or *authorised non-SRA firm*;

(VI) a member of an *LLP* which is a *recognised body*, *licensed body* or *authorised non-SRA firm*, or of an *LLP* which is a *manager* of a *recognised body*, *licensed body* or *authorised non-SRA firm*; or

(VII)a *partner* in a *partnership* with separate legal personality which is a *manager* of a *recognised body*, *licensed body* or *authorised non-SRA firm*;

(C) an *RFL* practising:

(I) as a *partner* in a *partnership* which is a *recognised body*, *licensed body* or *authorised non-SRA firm*, or in a *partnership* which should be a *recognised body* but has not been recognised by the *SRA*;

(II) as the *director* of a *company* which is a *recognised body*, *licensed body* or *authorised non-SRA firm*, or as the *director* of a *company* which is a *manager* of a *recognised body*, *licensed body* or *authorised non-SRA firm*;

(III) as a member of an *LLP* which is a *recognised body*, *licensed body* or *authorised non-SRA firm*, or as a member of an *LLP* which is a *manager* of a *recognised body*, *licensed body* or *authorised non-SRA firm*;

(IV) as a *partner* in a *partnership* with separate legal personality which is a *manager* of a *recognised body*, *licensed body* or *authorised non-SRA firm*;

(V) as an employee of a *recognised body*, *licensed body* or *recognised sole practice*; or

(VI) as an employee of a *partnership* which should be a *recognised body* but has not been authorised by the *SRA*, or of a *sole practitioner* whose *practice* should be a *recognised sole practice* but has not been authorised by the *SRA*;

(D) a *recognised body*;

(E) a *licensed body*;

(F) a *manager* or employee of a *recognised body* or *licensed body*, or of a *partnership* which should be a *recognised body* but has not been authorised by the *SRA*; or

(G) an employee in a *recognised sole practice*, or in a *sole practitioner* whose *practice* should be a *recognised sole practice* but has not been authorised by the *SRA*;

(vii) for the purposes of the *SRA Higher Rights of Audience Regulations* means a *solicitor* or an *REL*;

(viii) for the purposes of the *SRA Insolvency Practice Rules* means a *solicitor* or an *REL*;

(ix) for the purposes of the *SRA Quality Assurance Scheme for Advocates (Crime) Notification Regulations* means a *solicitor* or an *REL*; and

(x) for the purposes of the *SRA QASA Regulations* means a *solicitor* or an *REL*;

and references to "your" and "yourself" should be construed accordingly.

Rule 3: General Interpretation

3.1 Unless the context otherwise requires:

(a) the singular includes the plural and vice versa;

(b) words importing the masculine gender include the feminine and vice versa and references to the masculine or feminine include the neuter;

(c) the word "body" includes a *sole practitioner*, and a special body within the meaning of section 106 of the *LSA*;

(d) any explanatory notes, guidance notes and/or commentary are for the purposes of guidance only;

(e) any headings are for ease of reference only;

(f) any appendices to the provisions within the *SRA Handbook* will form part of the *SRA Handbook*;

(g) "in writing" includes any form of written electronic communication normally used for business purposes, such as emails;

(h) references to certificates, letters or other forms of written communication include references to those in both electronic and hard copy format; and

(i) a reference to any statute, statutory provision, code or regulation includes any subordinate legislation (as defined by section 21(1) of the Interpretation Act 1978) made under it.

[4] Holding client money and accounting to clients

[4.1] Solicitors Act 1974 (ss.34, 34A, 34B and 85)

[With consolidated amendments to 1 July 2009]

34. Accountants' reports

(1) The Society may make rules requiring solicitors to provide the Society with reports signed by an accountant (in this section referred to as an "accountant's report") at such times or in such circumstances as may be prescribed by the rules.

(2) The rules may specify requirements to be met by, or in relation to, an accountant's report (including requirements relating to the accountant who signs the report).

(3)–(5A) [*repealed*]

(6) If any solicitor fails to comply with the provisions of any rules made under this section, a complaint in respect of that failure may be made to the Tribunal by or on behalf of the Society.

(7)–(8) [*repealed*]

(9) Where an accountant, during the course of preparing an accountant's report –

- (a) discovers evidence of fraud or theft in relation to money held by a solicitor for a client or any other person (including money held on trust) or money held in an account of a client of a solicitor, or an account of another person, which is operated by the solicitor, or
- (b) obtains information which the accountant has reasonable cause to believe is likely to be of material significance in determining whether a solicitor is a fit and proper person to hold money for clients or other persons (including money held on trust) or to operate an account of a client of the solicitor or an account of another person,

the accountant must immediately give a report of the matter to the Society.

(10) No duty to which an accountant is subject is to be regarded as contravened merely because of any information or opinion contained in a report under subsection (9).

34A Employees of solicitors

(1) Rules made by the Society may provide for any rules made under section 31, 32, 33A or 34 to have effect in relation to employees of solicitors with such additions, omissions or other modifications as appear to the Society to be necessary or expedient.

(2) If any employee of a solicitor fails to comply with rules made under section 31 or 32, as they have effect in relation to the employee by virtue of subsection (1), any person may make a complaint in respect of that failure to the Tribunal.

(3) If any employee of a solicitor fails to comply with rules made under section 34, as they have effect in relation to the employee by virtue of subsection (1), a complaint in respect of that failure may be made to the Tribunal by or on behalf of the Society.

34B **Employees of solicitors: accounts rules etc**

(1) Where rules made under section 32(1) have effect in relation to employees of solicitors by virtue of section 34A(1), section 85 applies in relation to an employee to whom the rules have effect who keeps an account with a bank or building society in pursuance of such rules as it applies in relation to a solicitor who keeps such an account in pursuance of rules under section 32.

(2) Subsection (3) applies where rules made under section 32 –

- (a) contain any such provision as is referred to in section 33(1), and
- (b) have effect in relation to employees of solicitors by virtue of section 34A(1).

(3) Except as provided by the rules, an employee to whom the rules are applied is not liable to account to any client, other person or trust for interest received by the employee on money held at a bank or building society in an account which is for money received or held for, or on account of –

- (a) clients of the solicitor, other persons or trusts, generally, or
- (b) that client, person or trust, separately.

(4) Subsection (5) applies where rules made under section 33A(1) have effect in relation to employees of solicitors by virtue of section 34A(1).

(5) The Society may disclose a report on or information about the accounts of any employee of a solicitor obtained in pursuance of such rules for use –

- (a) in investigating the possible commission of an offence by the solicitor or any employees of the solicitor, and
- (b) in connection with any prosecution of the solicitor or any employees of the solicitor consequent on the investigation.

(6) Where rules made under section 34 have effect in relation to employees of solicitors by virtue of section 34A(1), section 34(9) and (10) apply in relation to such an employee as they apply in relation to a solicitor.

85. **Bank accounts**

Where a solicitor keeps an account with a bank or a building society in pursuance of rules under section 32 –

(a) the bank or society shall not incur any liability, or be under any obligation to make any inquiry, or be deemed to have any knowledge of any right of any person to any money paid or credited to the account, which it would not incur or be under or be deemed to have in the case of an account kept by a person entitled absolutely to all the money paid or credited to it; and

(b) the bank or society shall not have any recourse or right against money standing to the credit of the account, in respect of any liability of the solicitor to the bank or society, other than a liability in connection with the account.

[4.2] Legal Services Act 2007 (Designation as a Licensing Authority) (No.2) Order 2011, SI 2011/2866 (art.4)

Bank accounts of licensed bodies

4. (1) This article applies where a licensed body keeps an account with a bank or a building society in accordance with licensing rules made by the Society.

(2) The bank or building society –

(a) does not incur any liability;

(b) is not under any obligation to make any inquiry;

(c) is not deemed to have any knowledge of any right of any person to any money paid or credited to the account,

which it would not incur, or be under, or be deemed to have, in the case of an account kept by a person entitled absolutely to all the money paid or credited to it.

(3) The bank or building society has no recourse or right against money standing to the credit of the account, in respect of any liability of the licensed body to the bank or society, other than a liability in connection with the account.

(4) In this article –

(a) "bank" means –

(i) the Bank of England;

(ii) a person (other than a building society) who under Part 4 of the Financial Services and Markets Act 2000 has permission to accept deposits;

(iii) an EEA firm of the kind mentioned in paragraph 5(b) of Schedule 3 to that Act that has permission under paragraph 15 of that Schedule (as a result of qualifying for authorisation under paragraph 12(1) of that Schedule) to accept deposits; and

(b) "building society" means a building society incorporated (or deemed to be incorporated) under the Building Societies Act 1986.

[4.3] Law Society practice note: Holding client funds (extracts)[1]

[Last updated 29 April 2015]

2 Requirements under the Solicitors' Account Rules

[...]

Under rule 14.3 SAR you are required to return client money to your clients promptly – that is, as soon as there is no longer any proper reason to retain those funds. Payments received after you have already accounted to your client, for example by way of a refund, must also be paid to your client promptly. The rules do not define 'promptly' however, guidance note (vi) of rule 14 SAR guidance states that it should be given its natural meaning in the circumstances you find yourself.

2.1 *The purpose for retention*

It may sometimes be more convenient for your client for you to hold onto relevant funds than to return them if it is likely that you will need to use those funds to execute further instructions. For example, if your client is selling shares in a company following a buy-out, they might ask you to hold onto funds pending investment decisions on which you will be advising, or for other transactions in which you would be involved.

In these circumstances you should be aware of the rules governing client money, which aim to prohibit you as a solicitor from acting as a banker to your clients (see 2.5 below). [...]

2.5 *Solicitors as bankers*

The Solicitors Disciplinary Tribunal has determined that, as a solicitor, it is not a proper part of your everyday business or practice to operate a banking facility for third parties, whether or not they are your clients. As stated in guidance note (v) of rule 14 SAR, any exemption under the Financial Services and Markets Act 2000 (see section 3) is likely to be lost if a deposit is taken in circumstances which do not form part of your practice.

With this in mind, you should assess each case on its own merit based upon the individual circumstances that present themselves. If there is a good reason to continue to hold your client's money pending its investment or use in further transactions on which you continue to advise and act, it is unlikely that this would amount to a breach of the SAR. However, you should review this position if there is likely to be any significant delay in receiving further instructions.

1. See **www.lawsociety.org.uk** for future updates. The extracts set out here relate to SRA Accounts Rules 2011 (SAR), rules 14.3 (returning client money promptly); 14.4 (retaining client funds); 14.5 (not using client account as a banking facility); and associated notes (v)–(vii) to rule 14.

[...]

3 Exemption under the Financial Services and Markets Act 2000

Under the Financial Services and Markets Act 2000 (the Act) the Financial Services Authority (FSA) is the single statutory regulator of financial services business. Under the Act, if you undertake "regulated activities" you are required to either:

- be regulated by the FSA, or
- rely on the Part XX exemption

This exemption makes special provision for professional firms which do not carry on mainstream investment business but which may carry on regulated activities in the course of other work such as conveyancing, corporate, matrimonial, probate and trust work. This enables firms regulated by the SRA which meet certain conditions to be treated as exempt professional firms and to carry on activities known as exempt regulated activities.

[...]

If your firm qualifies for this exemption, you do not need to be regulated by the FSA, but will be able to carry on exempt regulated activities under the supervision of and regulation by the SRA. However, If you take a deposit from your client in circumstances which do not form part of your practice as a solicitor, you are likely to lose the exemption.

You should therefore ensure that the purpose for retention of your client's money is confirmed in writing and kept under review so that your exempt status is not placed at risk.

4 Money laundering

You should be cautious when being asked to hold onto sums of money by your client, and to be mindful that there are criminal sanctions against assisting money launderers. Please refer to our anti-money laundering practice note for further information in this area, and to assist you in meeting your obligations under the UK anti-money laundering and counter-terrorist financing regime.

[4.4] SRA guidance: Withdrawal of residual client balances

[Issued on 31 October 2014]

Status

Whilst this document does not form part of the SRA Handbook, the SRA may have regard to it when exercising its regulatory functions.

Who is this guidance relevant to?

This guidance is relevant to all practitioners who hold client money; Compliance Officers for Finance and Administration (COFAs); for firms that deal with client money and to accountants preparing applications on behalf of such firms.

Purpose of this guidance

Practitioners will often hold money on behalf of clients and although all client money will usually be used in the process of carrying out the retainer this is not always the case. This guidance is intended to assist when dealing with residual client balances (i.e. money due to clients where the client has become untraceable or where it has otherwise not been possible to return the money to the client) and designed to provide a framework that practitioners may find useful when dealing with such balances.

The SRA Principles

You must:

- act in the best interests of each client; (Principle 4)
- provide a proper standard of service to your clients; (Principle 5) and
- protect client money and assets. (Principle 10)

The SRA Rules

In these circumstances, the SRA Accounts Rules 2011 (Accounts Rules) require practitioners to return client money (including refunds received after the client has been accounted to) as soon as there is no longer a proper reason to retain that money (Rule 14.3). Therefore practitioners should, at the start of a retainer, consider how any residual balance that may arise will be returned and request appropriate information from clients, such as their national insurance number. The practitioner should also remind clients at the end of the retainer of their responsibility to provide them with an up to date address and contact details.

Imposing the obligation to return client money under rule [14.3] of the Accounts Rules goes to the heart of practitioners' duties. However, there are circumstances where it may not be possible for a practitioner to return client money. This may arise where the client has changed their contact details without notifying the practitioner, which further underlines the importance of returning client money as swiftly as possible.

Residual balances of £500 or less

Rule 20.1(j) of the Accounts Rules allows the withdrawal of residual client balances from the client account where the amount withdrawn does not exceed £500 in relation to any one individual client or trust matter and practitioners meet the criteria specified in Rule 20.2. The criteria requires practitioners to:

(a) establish the identity of the owner of the money, or make reasonable attempts to do so;

(b) make adequate attempts to ascertain the proper destination of the money, and to return it to the rightful owner, unless the reasonable costs of doing so are likely to be excessive in relation to the amount held;

(c) pay the funds to a charity;

(d) record the steps taken in accordance with the requirements above and retain those records, together with all relevant documentation (including receipts from the charity), in accordance with Rule 29.16 and 29.17(a); and

(e) keep a central register in accordance with Rule 29.22.

Residual balances above £500

Rule 20.1(k) allows practitioners to withdraw residual client balances above £500 from the client account and donate the money to a charity on the written authorisation of the Solicitors Regulation Authority (SRA). The SRA may impose a condition that the money is paid to a charity which gives an indemnity against any legitimate claim subsequently made for the sum received. In determining whether to grant authorisation, the SRA will assess the adequacy of the steps taken to identify the owner and return the funds.

Where it is intended that the money which is to be withdrawn from the client account is not going to be paid to a charity, for example, where a firm [wishes] to pay the money into the office account, it will still be necessary to make an application to the SRA. This situation might arise, for example, where it has not been possible for the practitioner to deliver a bill of costs because the client has become untraceable, with the consequence that the practitioner cannot make a transfer from client account to office account in accordance with Rules 17.2 and 17.3 of the Accounts Rules.

Furthermore, in relation to the administration of an estate or trust, it will normally be the executors, administrators or trustees, or the Court, who have authority to deal with unpaid money. Practitioners should therefore satisfy themselves as to any legal requirements in relation to their dealings with client money.

Establish the identity of the owner of the money, or make reasonable attempts to do so

What are reasonable steps to take in establishing the identity of the owner of client money will vary, depending on the situation. Factors affecting what will be considered reasonable include, but are not limited to:

- the age of the residual balance;
- the amount held;
- the client details available in respect of a balance and
- the costs associated with a particular tracing method.

Therefore, it is likely to be considered to be reasonable to require more intensive tracing efforts for larger or more recent residual balances, or for balances where more details are held about the client. Importantly practitioners should be aware that the absence of client details may highlight deficiencies in a firm's accounting practices and in the overall management and supervision of the firm as required by the outcomes in Chapter 7 of the SRA Code of Conduct.

The steps below provide a suggested framework for practitioners to employ when attempting to return residual client balances. However, it is worth highlighting that practitioners may identify other processes which also allow them to take reasonable steps to trace clients.

1. *Client file*

The client file is checked and all available contact details are used to try and contact the client or relevant third parties.

2. *Internet search*

An internet search is undertaken.

3. *Directory enquiries*

A Directory Enquiries search is undertaken.

4. *Electoral Register*

If a previous address is available for the client, an Electoral Register search is undertaken in the appropriate area.

5. *DWP letter forwarding service*

The Department for Work & Pensions (DWP) provides a tracing and letter forwarding service that can be used to forward beneficial information to clients where complete details are not held by the sender. The service costs less than £5 and has proved successful for many firms. This service can be utilised where you have an address or a previous address for the client. The letter may include a reference to the fact that monies are held for the client, but you should not include bills for forwarding to the client.

Companies House

If the balance belongs to a company, a Companies House search may be used to identify a current address if the company is still trading. Any monies due to a dissolved company pass to the Crown as bona vacantia and will be payable to the Treasury Solicitor under provisions in the Companies Act. Practitioners should clarify the situation with the Treasury Solicitor's Department before making an application to the SRA under Rule 20.1(k).

6. *Newspaper advertisement/tracing agent*

The cost of placing an advert in a newspaper (or other publication) or instructing a tracing agent will vary. However practitioners should still explore the cost implications of using these services if steps 1–6 above have proved unsuccessful and also take into account the likelihood of tracing the client using such methods, in the light of the information held about the client or third party to whom the monies are due.

Where the costs of placing an advertisement or instructing a tracing agent are unreasonable when compared with the balance in question, it is likely to be considered to be appropriate to withdraw a balance under £500 from the client account and pay the money to a charity.

Record Keeping

Practitioners are required to record the steps taken and retain those records, together with all relevant documentation (including receipts from the charity), in accordance with rule 29.16 and 29.17(a) and keep a central register in accordance with rule 29.22

Taken together, these rules require practitioners to:

- record the steps taken to try to identify the owner of the residual client balance and return the funds to them (including receipts from the recipient charity);
- keep a central register which details the
  - name of the client or other person or trust on whose behalf the money is held (if known),
  - residual balance amount,
  - name of the recipient charity,
  - date of payment.

Practitioners must retain these for at least six years from the date of the last entry.

Practitioners should not destroy files without client's consent and are advised not to archive files where a client balance remains, until such time as the balance is cleared.

When involved with mergers/acquisitions, acquiring firms are advised not to accept liability for existing client balances without taking receipt of the relevant files.

Practitioners' attention is drawn to the provisions of Rule 29.25 that makes clear firms should be able to justify the use of a suspension account and use of such an account must only be temporary.

Out-of-pocket expenses under £500

Solicitors have no legal authority to take out of pocket expenses. If such expenses are deducted the solicitor remains responsible to the client for these monies should they be traced. Such expenses, in all circumstances, should be reasonable expenses, for example; tracing agents' fees; advertisements; DWP searches, but would not include the administrative or office costs of the firm tracing the client or writing letters.

Where practitioners make an application to the SRA for authority to withdraw client money from a client account and incur out-of-pocket expenses, these can be taken into account by a decision maker, if the attempts to trace the client have not been successful.

Please note that if you make an application for authorisation to withdraw a residual client balance, the outcome will be available to other SRA business units. If the application is granted, details of the authorisation will also be publicly available if an enquiry is received by the SRA.

Further help

If you require further assistance in relation to your accounting requirements, contact us.[1]

To make an application for sums over £500 please complete our application form.[2]

1. See **Part 7** for contact details.
2. See **www.sra.org.uk/documents/rules/sar/sar-rule-20-1-k-application.doc.**

[4.5] SRA warning notice: Improper use of a client account as a banking facility

[Issued on 18 December 2014]

This notice is relevant to all regulated persons holding client monies, and must be read in conjunction with our four case studies on improper use of client account as a banking facility also published on 18 December 2014.[1]

The Solicitors Disciplinary Tribunal and the courts have sanctioned solicitors for many years for processing funds through client account for purposes unconnected with legal advice.

Since 1998, guidance note (ix) to Rule 15 of the Solicitors' Accounts Rules 1998 has warned solicitors of the need to exercise caution if asked to provide banking facilities through a client account and in 2004 the note was amended to state expressly that solicitors "should not provide banking facilities through a client account". In 2011, the guidance note was elevated to an Accounts Rule (Rule 14.5 of the SRA Accounts Rules 2011).

We have seen an increase in reports to us that client bank accounts are being used improperly as a banking facility, with its attendant risks of involvement in financial crime and the evasion of insolvency processes.

This guidance sets out a summary of the current position and some key issues that you should be aware of. We have also set out some case studies[2] to assist you in complying with your obligations.

Whilst this guidance does not form part of the SRA Handbook, we may have regard to it when exercising [our] regulatory functions.

Our rules/principles/outcomes

Rule 14.5 of the SRA Accounts Rules 2011 provides as follows:

> You must not provide banking facilities through a client account. Payments into, and transfers or withdrawals from, a client account must be in respect of instructions relating to an underlying transaction (and the funds arising therefrom) or to a service forming part of your normal regulated activities.

Guidance note (v) to Rule 14.5 states that:

> Rule 14.5 reflects decisions of the Solicitors Disciplinary Tribunal that it is not a proper part of a solicitor's everyday business or practice to operate a banking

1. See **4.6.**
2. See **4.6.**

facility for third parties, whether they are clients of the firm or not. It should be noted that any exemption under the Financial Services and Markets Act 2000 is likely to be lost if a deposit is taken in circumstances which do not form part of your practice. It should also be borne in mind that there are criminal sanctions against assisting money launderers.

The Principles

A breach of Rule 14.5 is a serious matter. In addition, allowing your firm's bank account to be used improperly may also involve a breach of the SRA Principles including:

- Principle 1: upholding the rule of law and the proper administration of justice;
- Principle 3: not allowing your independence to be compromised;
- Principle 6: behaving in a way that maintains the trust the public places in you and the provision of legal services; and
- Principle 8: running your business or carrying out your role in the business effectively and in accordance with proper governance and sound financial and risk management principles.

Outcome 7.5 of the SRA Code of Conduct 2011 also states that you must "comply with legislation applicable to your business, including anti-money laundering . . ."

Where clients ask you to process funds through your client account, you need to balance the client's best interests against the other Principles and your legal obligations. You should bear in mind note 2.2 to the Principles, which states that, where two or more Principles come into conflict, the Principle which takes precedence is the one which best serves the public interest in the particular circumstances, especially the public interest in the proper administration of justice and note 2.4 which states that compliance with the Principles is subject to any overriding legal obligations.

The Court of Appeal in The Attorney General for *Zambia* v. *Meer Care & Desai and others* [2008] EWCA Civ 1007 noted in paragraph 234:

> ... it is plain that he was providing the service of a bank account, albeit only in credit... with almost none of the payments through the client account being related to any legal work done by the firm. It is equally plain that this was not a proper thing for a firm of solicitors to do.

Recent High Court judgments

In the past two years, two High Court judgments have upheld the principles underlying Rule 14.5:

Premji Naram Patel v. SRA [2012] EWHC 3373 (Admin)

Mr Patel was a sole practitioner who acted for a company importing high value motor vehicles from Europe at a reduced price, to be sold in the UK for a substantial profit. Two significant investors were unwilling to pay funds directly to the company's owner because of past business failures. Instead investors paid money into the client account operated by Mr Patel. Mr Patel then transferred the relevant funds to the vehicle manufacturers directly.

We alleged that Mr Patel "permitted his bank account to be utilised by a client and/or third parties to receive and pay monies where there were no underlying legal transactions".

The Tribunal imposed a fine of £7,500.

Mr Patel appealed to the High Court. He argued that the second sentence of Rule 14.5 had to be read disjunctively: payments into and out of a client account have to relate to either (a) an underlying transaction or (b) a service forming part of the solicitor's normal regulated activities. He submitted that solicitors must not permit their client account to be used as a banking facility but will not be in breach of the rule if its use occurs as a consequence of a client's instructions in relation to an underlying transaction, albeit not a legal transaction.

The Court rejected that argument and upheld the fine imposed by the SDT commenting that "movements on client account must be in respect of instructions relating to an underlying transaction which is part of the accepted professional services of solicitors".

Fuglers & Ors v. SRA [2014] EWHC 179 (Admin) (QB)

Fuglers LLP acted for a Football Club. The Club's bank account was withdrawn after a winding-up petition was brought by HM Revenue & Customs (HMRC). The Club was insolvent.

Over a period of 4 months, approximately £10 million of the Club's money passed through Fuglers' client account.

The SDT fined Fuglers £50,000 and its two managers £5,000 and £20,000.

They appealed against the amount of the fines that were imposed. The High Court dismissed the appeal and confirmed the seriousness of the misconduct that had been found by the SDT.

At paragraphs 39 – 43, the Judge sets out three reasons why client accounts must not be used as banking facilities for clients:

- Objectionable in itself

  The first strand is that it is objectionable in itself for a solicitor to be carrying out or facilitating banking activities because he is to that extent not acting as a solicitor. If a solicitor is providing banking activities which are not linked to an underlying transaction, he is engaged in carrying out or facilitating day to day commercial trading in the same way as a banker. This is objectionable because solicitors are qualified and regulated in relation to their activities as solicitors, and are held out by the profession as being regulated in relation to such activities. They are not qualified to act as bankers and are not regulated as bankers. If a solicitor could operate a banking facility for clients which was divorced from any legal work being undertaken for them, he would in effect be trading on the trust and reputation which he acquired through his status as a solicitor in circumstances where such trust would not be justified by the regulatory regimen.

- Risk of money laundering

  The second strand is that allowing a client account to be used as a banking facility, unrelated to any underlying transaction which the solicitor is carrying out, carries with it the obvious risk that the account may be used unscrupulously by the client for money laundering. This was the danger referred to in paragraph 58 of the Tribunal decision in Wood and Burdett (8699/2002) which is referred to in note (ix) itself. That this was one of the dangers at which the rule was aimed is reinforced by the express mention in note (ix) of the criminal sanctions attaching to money laundering.

- Insolvency or risk of insolvency

The third strand arises in the particular context of insolvency or risk of insolvency. In such context, to allow a client account to be used as a banking facility is objectionable for several reasons. In the first place, it allows the client to achieve that which the client will normally be unable to achieve from any bank. It is the common practice of banks, as happened with the Club's bank in this case, to withdraw facilities upon notification that there has been a winding up petition. The solicitor is therefore giving the client a commercial service which would otherwise be unavailable to it through the device of using a solicitor as if he were a bank. Secondly there is the risk of disaffection and opprobrium which is involved in favouring one creditor over another. This exists in the absence of any risk of insolvency, but becomes more acute in the event of insolvency or potential insolvency. This arises irrespective of whether dispositions would or would not be subject to invalidity by the operation of section 127. A third reason is the risk of section 127 (of the Insolvency Act 1986) applying so as to require creditors to reimburse payments from the client account in a subsequent liquidation. A solicitor who knowingly makes or facilitates such payments may be subject to a personal liability, quite apart from the liability of the payee to reimburse the amount transferred.

Risks

You should therefore be aware that:

- **Providing banking facilities through a client account is objectionable in itself.**

For the avoidance of any doubt, our view is that you should only receive funds into client account in relation to an underlying transaction that you or your firm is advising on. It is not sufficient that there is an underlying transaction if you are not providing legal advice to one of the parties.

- **There must be a reasonable connection between the underlying legal transaction and the payments.**

Whether there is a reasonable connection is likely to depend on the facts of each case but where the legal services are purely advisory, it will clearly be more difficult to show a reasonable connection. The fact that you have a retainer with a client does not give you licence to process funds freely through client account on the client's behalf. Throughout a retainer, you should question why you are being asked to receive funds and for what purpose. You should only hold funds where necessary for the purpose of carrying out your client's instructions in connection with an underlying legal transaction or a service forming part of your normal regulated activities. You should always ask why the client cannot make the payment him or herself. The client's convenience is not the paramount concern and, if the client does not have a bank account in the UK, this considerably increases the risks. You should be prepared to justify any decision to hold or move client money to us where necessary.

- **Significant aggravating factors include the risks of insolvency and money laundering.**

The seriousness of the breach will be aggravated by indications that the funds were paid into, or transferred out of client account, to avoid responsibilities imposed by insolvency legislation or to perpetuate suspected financial crime or tax fraud. In the case of Simms SDT 8686/2002 the Tribunal noted at paragraph 76:

> A solicitor who involves himself in transactions which he knows or suspects or should have known or suspected could involve illegality or impropriety or who gives such transactions credibility cannot but appreciate that his behaviour will be perceived as affecting his integrity and trustworthiness and so affect the reputation of the Profession. The duties of a lawyer as an officer of The Supreme Court are not simply owed to the client but also involve the respect which the Profession owes to the law itself and to justice.

You should be aware that criminals often target solicitors' client accounts to lend credibility to fraudulent schemes or to launder the proceeds of their criminal activity. You must not allow money to move through client account unless it is in connection with a genuine transaction about which you are providing legal services. You should ensure that you undertake proper due diligence before accepting any funds into client account and you should not act if you do not fully understand the transaction on which you are advising.

Compliance with Rule 14.5 offers an important "first line of defence" to clients who may seek to take advantage of your client account to launder money. It also helps you to secure professional independence from your client in compliance with Principle 3.

You should make sure that you and all members of your firm are familiar with the warning notices and guidance we have issued in relation to high yield investment fraud and money laundering.

Other related issues/considerations

Use of escrow accounts

Firms may hold funds "in escrow" or subject to professional undertakings in circumstances where they are advising a party to the underlying legal transaction; for example, funds for the purchase of an asset (e.g. an aircraft) might be held pending the completion of a purchase.

The decision of the SDT in Wilson-Smith (SDT 8772/2003) (para 60) was unequivocal that a solicitor should not act as "escrow only" agent:

> It can be described as nothing other than crass stupidity to accept a role as, for example, an "escrow agent" when the solicitor cannot know what that means as, indeed, that expression has no meaning in English law.

The use of escrow accounts is a serious risk if they do not have a reasonable connection to an underlying legal transaction (which you are advising on) or are not in association with the recognised "professional duties" of a solicitor. For the avoidance of doubt, if you are instructed only to advise on the terms of an escrow account in the absence of being instructed on an underlying legal transaction or the provision of other professional duties (such as probate services), this is likely to involve a breach of Rule 14.5.

In each case you must therefore carefully consider all of the relevant circumstances and the risks involved before you agree to hold funds in escrow. You should be prepared to justify your decision to us where necessary.

A possible alternative: If parties want funds to be held independently in escrow, they could appoint an independent trustee company or bank regulated by the FCA and authorised to provide banking and/or escrow services.

Private client services

Historically, some solicitors have agreed to receive and hold funds for clients to enable them to pay routine bills and invoices on their clients' behalf. This has been predominately for the clients' convenience as they may be based abroad or because they are incapacitated so that operating their own bank accounts is problematic.

In view of technological advancements, in particular the ease of internet and telephone banking, we consider that allowing client account to be used in this way is no longer appropriate. Clients can now operate their bank accounts from their own homes or indeed from anywhere in the world. Allowing clients to hold anonymously what might be significant funds in a client account gives rise to significant risks in relation to potential money laundering or other breaches of the law, such as exchange control consent regulation. The anonymity of client accounts is attractive to criminals.

In each case, you must therefore carefully consider all of the relevant circumstances and the risks involved before you agree to hold funds in this way. You should be prepared to justify your decision to us where necessary.

This guidance is not intended to affect your ability to make reasonable and proper payments on your client's instructions when related to an underlying legal transaction on which you have been instructed, for example, upon completion of a house purchase on your client's instructions under Accounts Rule 20.1(f). Once a transaction is complete, we would remind you that Rule 14.3 provides that client money must be returned to the client promptly, as soon as there is no longer any proper reason to retain those funds. If you retain funds in client account after completion of a transaction, the risk of a breach of Rule 14.5 increases. Risk factors of laundering in particular would involve the payment of substantial sums to others, including family members, or to corporate entities, particularly overseas, since there is no reason why the client could not receive the money into their own account and transfer it from there.

Enforcement action

Failure to comply with this warning notice may lead to disciplinary action.

Further help

- **High-yield investment fraud: Warning notice.** Issued on 10 September 2013
- **Money laundering and terrorist financing: Warning notice.** Issued on 8 December 2014

Further assistance

If you require further assistance with understanding your obligations in relation to anything please contact the Professional Ethics Guidance Team.[3]

3. See **Part 7**.

[4.6] SRA case studies: Improper use of client account as a banking facility

[18 December 2014]

The case studies below should be read in conjunction with our warning notice on improper use of client account as a banking facility, also issued on 18 December 2014.[1]

Case study 1

A solicitor acted for an upmarket bathroom and kitchen company which required customers to pay a 33% deposit on the purchase price. The customers were concerned that the company could become insolvent and wanted to pay the money to the company's solicitor to hold on the customer's behalf. The solicitor agreed to accept the funds from customers, to be held in general client account, and paid out when certain conditions in the escrow agreement were fulfilled. Over £2.2 million was paid into and out of client account in this way over a 15 month period. The solicitor advised the company on the initial terms of the standard escrow agreement and on a minor employment issue 6 months ago but otherwise provided no other legal advice. The solicitor charged a monthly fee for this service.

In our view, this arrangement breaches Rule 14.5. The facts fall within the Court's decision in Patel and the solicitor should not have agreed to accept the funds in this way.

Case study 2

A firm was instructed to act as execution only escrow agent in a proposed investment transaction. The firm's retainer was purportedly limited to reviewing the terms of the escrow agreement and releasing funds in accordance with it. The retainer letter excluded any advice on the underlying transaction and the firm made no attempt to understand the underlying transaction; it simply received and distributed escrow funds of over £650,000. According to the client's instructions to the firm, the underlying transaction involved investment in foreign currency bearer bonds. A subsequent investigation showed that there appeared to have been no genuine underlying legal transaction and the transaction displayed several of the warning signs from the SRA's warning notice on money laundering.

In our view, this breaches Rule 14.5 as the firm agreed to act as "escrow only" agent without advising on any underlying transaction. Breaches of the Principles, Code of Conduct and the Money Laundering Regulations are also likely to be involved. In the SRA's experience, the use of purported "limited retainers" is often in itself a red flag because a firm is actually aware that a transaction is suspicious and is seeking to avoid addressing its nature.

1. See **4.5**.

Case study 3

A solicitor acted for a wealthy client living abroad who owned a personal residential property in central London and a portfolio of commercial properties. In respect of both, only very limited legal services were provided, such as the provision of property tax advice and general representative duties. Most of the services centred around paying utility and other bills for the private property and receiving in client account, and then holding, commercial tenancy deposits. The client did not instruct the solicitor on the preparation of the commercial leases, using instead a property agent. The client put the solicitor in significant funds on a periodic basis for payment of the utility bills and other outgoings and also for his UK tax liabilities; in excess of £300,000 a year. All transactions passed through the firm's client bank account.

In our view, although arguably the payment of the client's personal tax liabilities may have been sufficiently connected with the tax advice being given to him, payment of the utility bills was not. As there was no ongoing advice on the leases, it is questionable whether it was appropriate to agree to hold the commercial tenancy deposits in client account. The only rationale the solicitor could advance for this was that the client had asked him to do so for his administrative convenience. In our view, the solicitor should not have agreed to act in this way and in doing so has breached Rule 14.5.

Case study 4

A firm acted for a property development company. The original retainer related to a redevelopment of a block of flats, the creation of separate leasehold interests and sale of the individual leases. When the flats were sold, the client asked the firm to retain the proceeds in the firm's client account. The company then asked the firm to make a series of payments from client account, using the proceeds of sale from the first development: to pay a building contractor, architect and council tax in relation to another development site and to pay £56,000 to a consultant for his services as a sales agent. The consultant asked the firm to split the payment, paying £9,000 to a car dealership as a deposit on a new car and the balance to another firm of solicitors as a deposit on a property he was purchasing. The firm was not instructed to provide legal advice in connection with the development site. Its role was limited to making the requested payments. The firm later found out that the consultant was in the process of going through a divorce.

In our view, all of these payments are in breach of Rule 14.5. To minimise the risk of committing a breach of Rule 14.5, the firm should have returned the sale proceeds to its client at the end of the initial retainer. The payments requested by the consultant exposed the firm to the risk of sheltering funds in a matrimonial dispute.

[4.7] SRA warning notice: Money missing from client account

[Issued on 12 June 2015]

Status

Whilst this document does not form part of the SRA Handbook, we may have regard to it when exercising our regulatory functions.

Who is this notice relevant to?

This warning notice is aimed at all those we regulate but is particularly relevant to you if you are a manager of a firm or a firm's COFA or COLP.

Any deficiency on client account exposes clients and others to a risk of financial loss and damage to public confidence. Missing money must be replaced with extreme urgency.

The Solicitors Regulation Authority's Principles

You have a duty to ensure that client money is safe. Operating a deficient client account may cause you to breach one or more of the SRA Principles, including:

- Principle 2 – acting with integrity
- Principle 5 – acting in the best interests of each client;
- Principle 6 – behaving in a way that maintains the trust the public places in you and in the provision of legal services;
- Principle 10 – protecting client money and assets.

The Solicitors Regulation Authority's mandatory outcomes

You should also have regard to the following mandatory Outcomes:

O(1.1) You treat your clients fairly;

O(1.2) You provide services to your clients in a manner which protects their interests in their matter, subject to the proper administration of justice;

O(1.12) Clients are in a position to make informed decisions about the services they need, how their matter will be handled and the options available to them;

O(1.16) You inform current clients if you discover any act or omission which could give rise to a claim by them against you.

O(4.2) Any individual who is advising a client makes that client aware of all information material to that retainer of which the individual has personal knowledge.

SRA Accounts Rules 2011

It is your duty to remedy breaches of the SRA Accounts Rules 2011. Specifically Rule 7 states:

> 7.1 Any breach of the rules must be remedied promptly upon discovery. This includes the replacement of any money improperly withheld or withdrawn from a client account.
>
> 7.2 In a private practice, the duty to remedy breaches rests not only on the person causing the breach, but also on all the principals in the firm. This duty extends to replacing missing client money from the principals' own resources, even if the money has been misappropriated by an employee or another principal, and whether or not a claim is subsequently made on the firm's insurance or the Compensation Fund.

The implications of missing money

It is important that all managers and employees of a firm fully understand the implications of money being missing from client account, including:

- There is a clear duty in the SRA Accounts Rules to replace a deficiency in a client account.
- In the general law, trustees in breach of trust also have a duty to replace a deficiency.
- In any event, operating a deficient client account is very likely to involve immediate and continuing breaches of trust – by paying some clients their full entitlement, the amount left for other clients reduces.
- Ultimately, a deficient trust account is likely to be distributed pro rata.
- You may well breach your duty to act in the best interests of clients if you pay client money into an already deficient account without fully informed consent – no properly advised client would pay funds into a deficient account with the risk of only receiving a proportion back. Failing to inform clients exposes them to a risk of loss (see O 4.2).
- Until missing money is replaced, you should not take costs from the client account – you cannot "properly" require payment of your fees from money held in a client account in such circumstances and so rules 17.2 and 17.3 of the SRA Accounts Rules 2011 will not apply. Nor is it in the best interests of clients for you to take costs from client account when there is insufficient in the account for you to pay them in full.
- If you or your insurers do not replace the money promptly, you are at serious risk of intervention by the SRA. Intervention may be necessary in any event if there is reason to suspect dishonesty or other grounds for intervention arise.
- Since it is unlikely that a deficient client account can be operated without further breach of trust, you may well need to apply to the court for directions as to how to distribute the remaining funds.

- Offences under the Fraud Act 2006 may be committed once you are on notice that money is missing if you do not act properly and honestly.

Complying with the Principles

It is critical that to protect your clients, you do not operate a deficient client account and that you keep client money safe.

If you are the firm's COFA, you must take all reasonable steps to ensure compliance with the SRA Accounts Rules 2011 and record any failure to comply. You also have an obligation to report material breaches to the SRA as soon as reasonably practicable.

If you are a manager, the COFA is not a substitute for you and your firm's responsibilities and obligations. Systems and actions that should aid compliance include:

- having appropriate accounting procedures for your business;
- having clear reporting lines to encourage appropriate reporting by all members of staff;
- ensuring that your systems only allow appropriate individuals to authorise payments from client account;
- immediately investigating and taking action against any member of staff who may have acted dishonestly or committed any financial impropriety whether in relation to client account or not;
- taking regular steps to monitor, review and manage risks.

Behaviours of concern that you should be alert to in your firm include:

- failure to deliver bills or provide written notification of costs;
- any suggestions of overcharging;
- borrowing from clients in the capacity of trustee or attorney, which is unsecured;
- borrowing that remains outstanding, in breach of any agreement to pay;
- delay or failure to account for monies due;
- any accumulation or pattern of one or more of the above.

If you identify that money is missing

If you identify that money is missing, you have a duty to take steps to ensure it is replaced, in full, immediately.

If you are a manager of the firm, you have a duty to replace missing client money from your own resources. It may be necessary for you to obtain a loan to do this. It is irrelevant that fault may not lie with you personally.

You may be able to make a claim on your professional indemnity insurance. The obligation to remedy a breach of the SRA Accounts Rules 2011 is treated as civil liability for the purposes of clause 1 of the Minimum Terms and Conditions.

Operating the client account when it is deficient may make you liable for breach of trust and failure to act in the best interests of your clients. If you cannot replace the missing money and your insurers do not do so very promptly, you may be unable lawfully to operate the account. You will have to consider the position as a matter of trust law including whether you need to apply to court for directions as trustee.

Enforcement action

Whilst we are committed to working constructively with you, we will take enforcement action if missing money is not replaced. Failure to replace missing money will usually lead to an intervention. It should not be assumed that replacing the money means that an intervention is not necessary since the conduct giving rise to the shortage may evidence dishonesty or other breaches giving rise to a need to intervene to protect clients and the public.

Further assistance

If you require further assistance with understanding your obligations in relation to anything please contact the Professional Ethics Guidance Team.

[4.8] Law Society practice note: Protection for client accounts[1]

[Last updated 6 January 2016]

1 Introduction

1.1 *Who should read this practice note?*

All solicitors handling client accounts.

1.2 *What is the issue?*

This practice note sets out good practice in the event of an authorised deposit-taking institution collapse. Funds held on behalf of clients could be affected and may be eligible for compensation. Following changes to the rules governing payout of compensation in such an event, the Financial Services Compensation Scheme (FSCS) has introduced new processes and technology to enable faster payout.

This practice note provides information on the framework governing deposit protection and provides best practice advice for practitioners.

2 Liability for client money following institution collapse

It is unlikely that you will be liable in negligence if client money is lost following the collapse of a deposit-taking institution, as long as you have placed the money in accordance with the Solicitors' Accounts Rules (SARs). However, any final decision would be for the courts.

Any express undertakings you have made to pay money must be honoured, even if the institution with which they were deposited has collapsed.

2.1 *SRA Solicitors Accounts Rules 2011 (SARs)*

You must place client money in a client account at a bank or building society, as defined in section 87 of the Solicitors Act 1974. These institutions must have permission from the Financial Conduct Authority (FCA) to accept deposits. A client account must be held at a branch or a head office in England and Wales – Rule 13(4) SARs.

You must ensure that your clients gain a reasonable rate of interest on their money, but you do not need to obtain the best rate (See rules 22–23 SARs).

You should check the interest rates paid on client accounts and consider whether it is appropriate to change deposit-taking institutions in the light of the deals available. In deciding, you should consider factors, such as access to the money, the administrative

1. See **www.lawsociety.org.uk** for future updates.

costs of changing deposit-taking institution and whether the new deposit-taking institution is covered by the FSCS.

The SARs do not prevent you from:

- dividing money among separate client accounts, or
- distributing client money in different deposit taking institutions.

2.2 *Terms of business*

You may also state in your terms of business that if you make a claim under the FSCS in respect of client money on your clients' behalf, you will, subject to their consent, give certain client information to the FSCS to help them identify clients and any amounts to which they are entitled.

3 Financial Services Compensation Scheme (FSCS)

The FSCS is the UK's statutory compensation scheme for customers of financial services firms. The FSCS can pay compensation to consumers if a company is unable, or likely to be unable, to pay claims against it.

Under European Deposit Guarantee Scheme Directive (DGSD), and corresponding UK legislation, compensation limit for eligible claimants in the event of failure of a deposit-taking firm is £75,000 (equivalent to the €100,000 compensation limit set out in DGSD).

The FSCS is required to pay deposit compensation for verified claims where the account holder is not absolutely entitled to the eligible deposit within three months of the failure of a deposit taking institution. However, the FSCS aims to pay within 20 working days wherever possible.

3.1 *Eligibility criteria*

Eligible claimants include individuals, small and large companies, and small local authorities (such as parish councils).

Large companies and small local authorities are newly included for cover under FSCS desposit protection. They are eligible for compensation up to the new limit of £75,000.

3.2 *Considerations for client accounts*

The FSCS deposit-protection scheme applies to client money in the same way as it applies to private/individual deposits. Therefore the FSCS protects the first £75,000 deposited, with an authorised deposit-taking institution, on behalf of a client. Note that the £75,000 FSCS limit applies to the individual client, and so if they hold other personal monies themselves in the same deposit-taking institution as your client account, the limit remains £75,000 in total for that individual.

You do not need to write to the deposit-taking institution to confirm that an account was opened on behalf of clients. Deposit-taking institutions will know this from your application to open the account, particularly as the account must have the word "client" in its title according to Rule 13(3) of the SARs.

It is important to note that the protection only applies per banking licence. Some authorised deposit-taking institutions have several brands that are covered by one banking licence. Therefore it is possible to have money deposited with several deposit-taking institution brands but for them to be covered by only one licence. In these circumstances only the first £75,000 is protected for each individual.

Mergers and takeovers in recent years have complicated the picture significantly. It may be useful for you to ascertain whether the accounts you hold client money in are covered by one banking licence or several.

3.3 *Accounts in foreign deposit-taking institutions*

The recast DGSD has standardised the limit across all EU member states to €100,000 (or its equivalent). The directive states that, where a deposit taker fails that has branches in another EU member state, the "home" state scheme must introduce the "host" state scheme to make payment to the branch depositors on its behalf. In this event the payment would be made in the currency of the "host" state.

3.4 *Temporary High Balances*

The FSCS now provides a £1m protection limit for temporary high balances held with a bank, building society or credit union if it fails. Cover is related to specific life events and limited to natural persons only.

The change comes from the recast DGSD. People with some types of temporary high balances will have FSCS protection for up to £1m for up to six months. Proceeds resulting from the following life events are categorised as temporary high balances:

Sums paid to the depositor in respect of:

- Real estate transactions (property purchase, sale proceeds, equity release) relating to a depositor's main or only residence
- Benefits payable under an insurance policy
- Personal injury compensation (unlimited amount)
- Disability or incapacity (state benefits)
- Claims for compensation for wrongful conviction
- Claim for compensation for unfair dismissal
- Redundancy (voluntary or compulsory)
- Marriage or civil partnership
- Divorce or dissolution of civil partnership
- Benefits payable on retirement
- Benefits payable on death
- A claim for compensation in respects of a person's death
- Inheritance
- Proceeds of a deceased's estate held by their Personal Representative

Deposits over £75,000 are protected up to six months from when the amount was first credited or from the moment a qualifying deposit became legally transferrable. "Temporary" means that the deposit must have been credited to the account (or become legally transferable if that is later) no more than six months before the firm goes into default.

4 Actions for making compensation claims

If a deposit-taking institution collapses, you should:

1. Contact the FSCS with details of all clients whose money is held in an account with the collapsed deposit-taking institution, including their full name and address details.

2. Tell the FSCS the amount in the account to which each client is entitled (with supporting evidence).

3. Ensure that you inform FSCS whether monies held in a client account are due to be paid to the Legal Services Commission or are held on trust for a third party who is not your client.

You must seek the consent of your clients before providing the FSCS with the details described in 1 and 2 above. If an individual client does not give consent, the FSCS will still need to know the account balances, but you may withhold the identity of the client. In this latter case, the client will not be able to receive compensation from the FSCS.

The need for consent may delay the payment of compensation beyond the 20-day payment threshold, depending on how quickly it can be ascertained by you.

4.1 *Providing information to the FSCS*

The FSCS has created a template excel spreadsheet for completing the information required. The template can be downloaded from the FSCS website. Once complete, it should be emailed to **beneficiaries@fscs.org.uk.**

You may have a general client account into which you deposit the monies of a number of clients. You may even have a number of general client accounts within one or across many deposit-taking institutions. One template spreadsheet should be completed for each client account.

4.1.1 *Single client accounts*

In cases where there is one account per client and a deposit-taking institution becomes insolvent (requiring the FSCS to pay compensation) it should be relatively straight forward to identify the client and the amount to be refunded, subject to the amount being less than or equal to the compensation limit.

4.1.2 *Multiple client accounts*

In cases of several client accounts a separate template must be completed for each account. If you have records of where each individual client's money is held you should notify the FSCS of the following details:

- the amount held on behalf of the affected client
- their entitlement to the funds in the relevant account, and
- their contact details

This information should be clear from your accounting records. You must ensure that you have the consent of your client to pass on these details to the FSCS.

In some cases it may be difficult to identify which individual client's money is held in which general client account. In such cases the FSCS will still expect you to fill out a template for each account held with the insolvent institution detailing the individual amounts of money held on behalf of each client in the affected client account or accounts.

4.2 *Seeking additional funds*

You may need to seek additional funds from clients according to the proportion of the total funds held in the failed deposit-taking institution if you are to complete transactions for them before they receive compensation.

5 Information for your client

Informing your client about how their money is held will help you manage the situation following the collapse of a deposit-taking institution.

You may do the following:

- Explain it is unlikely that you will be held liable for losses resulting from a banking failure.
- Tell them the name of the deposit-taking institution in which their money is held.
- Explain that the £75,000 FSCS limit applies to the individual client, and so if they hold other personal monies themselves in the same deposit-taking institution as your client account, the limit remains £75,000 in total.
- Tell them that some deposit-taking institutions have several brands, ie where the same institution is trading under different names. Clients should check either with their deposit-taking institution, the FCA or a financial adviser for more information.
- Seek consent for the disclosure to FSCS of client details in the event of a deposit-taking institution failure.

6 Qualified undertakings

Some solicitors have asked whether they can offer qualified undertakings.

You are free to decide whether to offer or accept an undertaking, so long as to do so is not against the client's interests. You do not need to give an undertaking simply because it is in the client's interests to do so. You may also negotiate the terms of the undertakings, where this is in the best interests of clients.

However, in residential conveyancing transactions, it is highly unlikely that buyers' solicitors could properly accept offers of a limited undertaking in their clients' best interest. Also, offering such an undertaking may breach the obligations of sellers' solicitors to their clients, depending on the terms of their retainer.

For further information on conveyancing undertakings to discharge mortgages see:

- Chapter 11 of the SRA Code: Relations with third parties and specifically, Outcome 11.2 and Indicative Behaviours 11.5 and 11.6.
- *Conveyancing Handbook*, 22nd edition. The relevant sections are section E.3, F.4 and the guidance on accepting undertakings after *Patel* v. *Daybells* [2001] EWCA Civ 1229 in appendix VI.6.

7 More information

7.1 *Further advice*

7.1.1 PRACTICE ADVICE LINE

The Law Society provides support for solicitors on a wide range of areas of practice. Practice advice can be contacted on 020 7320 5675 from 09:00 to 17:00 on weekdays.

7.1.2 LAW SOCIETY CONSULTING

If you require further support, Law Society Consulting can help. We offer expert and confidential support and guidance, including face-to-face consultancy on risk and compliance and finance and accounting. Please contact us on 020 7316 5655, or complete the relevant form.

7.1.3 OTHER

Solicitors Regulation Authority's Professional Ethics Helpline for advice on conduct issues.

The FCA provides the following information:

- Financial Conduct Authority/FCA money made clear
- FCA Handbook

The Financial Services Compensation Scheme (FSCS) is the UK's compensation fund of last resort for customers of authorised financial services firms.

- Financial Services Compensation Scheme

[5] Charging clients and paying tax

[5.1] Law Society practice note: Publicising solicitors' charges (extracts)[1]

[Last updated 15 September 2015]

2 Providing clear and accurate information

Clients should not be led to believe that costs are likely to be less than they will be and headline prices should be presented in a manner that enables "like for like" comparisons in terms of cost information, with breakdowns of charges where appropriate.

2.1 *Publicising fixed and estimated charges*

Publicising your charges should help your clients make an informed decision as to whether to instruct your firm based on what the final charge is likely to be. Failing to provide the appropriate level of detail may be considered to be misleading, and you could be in breach of Outcome 1.1 of the SRA Code, to treat your client fairly.

Outcome 8.1 of the SRA Code states that you must ensure that any publicity provided by your firm must not be misleading or inaccurate. Outcome 8. 2 states that publicity relating to your firm's charges must be clearly expressed, and must state whether disbursements and VAT are included in the quoted sum.

To comply with these outcomes you should avoid the following practices:

- estimating charges pitched at an unrealistically low level (IB 8.7)
- advertising additional "sundries" or "catch all" amounts for such without providing details about the purpose of the charges
- providing estimated or fixed charges plus disbursements, if expenses which are in the nature of overheads are then charged as disbursements
- providing estimated or fixed charges for conveyancing services which may require additional charges for work on a related mortgage loan or repayment, including work done for a lender, unless the publicity makes it clear that additional charges may be payable (e.g. by including a clear statement such as "excluding VAT, disbursements, mortgage related charges and charges for work done for a lender")

These terms apply to all publicised costs, including those publicised via the internet and online services.

[...]

1. These extracts focus on publicising a firm's charges, including disbursements, generally; for further detail, refer to the full practice note at **www.lawsociety.org.uk**. The annex at **5.2** deals specifically with charging for telegraphic transfer fees.

2.3 VAT and disbursements

When giving an estimate or quotation for charges, you should make it clear to your client whether or not VAT and disbursements are included in the quoted sum (Outcome 8.2). Quotes should be as comprehensive as possible. Where VAT is not mentioned, it should be presumed that the sum is VAT inclusive.

[...]

3 Disbursements

3.1 *Definition*

"Disbursements" are defined by the Solicitors' Accounts Rules 2011 (SAR) as any sum that you spend or are going to spend on behalf of your client or trust, including any VAT element.

You should not charge for items as disbursements when they do not amount to such. You should also refrain from increasing the amount of a disbursement by adding on an element of fees while representing the total amount as a disbursement. The information you provide should be clear to enable clients to make an informed decision. You should be clear about what amounts to the headline figure, any other fees and disbursements and explain what any other fees relate to so that clients can understand if another solicitor has included them in their headline figure.

[...]

3.3 *Additional charges*

Items that relate to your firm's charges are not disbursements and should not be described as such. These items are typically part of a normal conveyancing transaction and so can be charged as fees, or form part of your firm's overheads.

[5.2] Law Society practice note: Telegraphic transfer fees (extracts)

[Last updated 30 July 2008]

1 Introduction

[...]

1.2 *What is the issue?*

A recent Solicitors Disciplinary Tribunal (SDT) decision found against the partners of a practice for concealing profit costs from their clients by referring to a telegraphic transfer fee as a disbursement.

2 Charging for telegraphic transfers

2.1 *What is a disbursement?*

The SRA Accounts Rules 2011 define a disbursement as "an expense".

2.2 *Is a telegraphic transfer fee a disbursement?*

A TT fee is an expense but some practices charge more than the cost of the transfer under the heading disbursement, thereby concealing profit costs from clients.

The SDT has found that this clearly breaches rule 1 of the code of conduct, particularly in relation to the solicitor's duty to act with integrity and in the best interests of the client.

This conduct is also likely to be in breach of rule 2, client care, if any amount over the cost of the transfer is not explicitly declared to the client as profit costs.

2.3 *How should telegraphic transfers be charged?*

You must advise the client of the basis and terms of your charges.

You should tell your client that you are charging them the fee that has been charged to the practice by the financial institution executing the telegraphic transfer, and that this fee is a disbursement.

You must charge VAT on the fee that has been charged to the practice by the financial institution executing the telegraphic transfer, even if no VAT is charged to you. For more information see Costs passed on to clients – disbursements – and VAT on the HM Revenue and Customs website.

You must not include any profit cost element as a disbursement. For example, you must not include a fixed monthly charge by the bank for having an in-house terminal, or any internal staff costs.

If you charge the client an administration fee for arranging the telegraphic transfer you must inform the client and charge it as profit cost.

3 The Solicitors Disciplinary Tribunal (SDT) ruling

An SDT case reported in June 2008 clearly demonstrates the implications of referring to a mixed charge partially comprising a profit costs element and including a telegraphic transfer fee as "a disbursement".

3.1 *The facts*

The practice charged the client £30 plus VAT for a TT as a disbursement. The practice only paid £10 to its bank for each TT.

The client care letter sent to clients under rule 15 (now rule 2) of the code of conduct did not explain that the practice would only pay on £10 and that the balance amounted to profit costs for the practice.

It did not explain that the additional fee related to work undertaken in arranging the TT.

3.2 *The allegations*

Claiming the TT fee as a disbursement of £30 was misleading to the client. The balance over the actual disbursement was additional income and profit to the practice.

3.3 *The findings*

- The respondents had acted in breach of rule 1 and rule 2 of the code of conduct.
- The practice's invoices did not reflect the telegraphic transfer fee and the true position was not addressed in the letters addressed to the clients. The clients had therefore been misled.
- A fee charged to the client by the practice had been described as a disbursement met by the practice which was inaccurate. This hid the fee for handling a transfer in addition to the bank's charges.
- In all of the circumstances of the case, the STD considered it appropriate and proportionate to fine each respondent £1,500.

[5.3] Law Society practice note: VAT on disbursements (extracts)[1]

[Last updated 10 March 2011]

6 Counsel's fees: concessionary treatment

A concessionary treatment for counsel's fees paid into and kept in client account was agreed between HMCE [HM Customs and Excise, the predecessor to HM Revenue and Customs], the Bar Council and the Law Society at the time VAT was first introduced (this was published in the *Gazette* on 4 April 1973).

There are two ways in which you may treat counsel's fees:

6.1 *Method (i)*

You may treat the fee as your own expense and thus reclaim the VAT element as input tax. When you deliver your own bill of costs to your client, the value of the supply for VAT purposes is the value of your own costs, plus the tax *exclusive* value of counsel's fees.

EXAMPLE

Assume your professional charges are £1,200 plus £240 VAT (assuming a rate of 20 per cent), and the bill includes unpaid counsel's fees of £800, plus £160 VAT. The £160 VAT on counsel's fee note is treated as your input tax and can be reclaimed by you from HMRC. Your bill should show:

Legal services	£1,200.00	
Counsel's fees	£800.00	
		£2,000.00
VAT @ 20%		£400.00
TOTAL		£2,400.00

When payment of £2,400 is received, the Solicitors Accounts Rules provide that the sum may either:

- be paid into an office account at a bank or building society in England and Wales; by the end of the second working day following receipt, the amount due to counsel of £960 (£800 plus VAT of £160) must either be paid out of office account or be transferred to client account pending payment; or
- be split between client account and office account as appropriate, or be paid into

1. References to the SRA Accounts Rules 2011, effective from 6 October 2011, are shown here in square brackets. See **www.lawsociety.org.uk** for future updates.

client account with a transfer out of client account of office monies (£1,200 costs and £400 VAT) within 14 days of receipt.

[SRA Accounts Rules 2011, rule 17.1(b) and rule 18] – the option in rule [17.1(b)] may be used only if the payment includes no client money other than professional disbursements incurred but not yet paid.

Because counsel's fee is being treated for VAT purposes as an expense of the solicitor and the VAT element is being reclaimed by you, payment, when it is made, must be from the office account, so that the appropriate entry can be made in the VAT ledger account. At that stage the sum held in client account can be transferred to the office account.

6.2 *Method (ii)*

You may treat counsel's advice as supplied directly to your client and the settlement of the fees as a disbursement for VAT purposes. Counsel's VAT invoice (receipted fee note) may be amended by

- inserting on the fee note your client's name and the word "per" immediately preceding your own name and address; or
- crossing out your name and address and replacing it with the name and address of your client.

The fee note from counsel will then be recognised as a valid VAT invoice in the hands of your client (who can reclaim the VAT if registered) and no VAT record need be kept in your accounts ledgers. You should keep a photocopy of the VAT invoice.

Where you consider that the services of counsel, if supplied directly to the client, would be outside the scope of UK VAT, you must *not* certify counsel's fee note to this effect and pay counsel only the fee net of VAT. You may advise counsel that VAT is not due on their services because of the place of belonging of the client. You may provide them with appropriate commercial evidence of the client's place of belonging.

Where the client is in business in other EU Member States, this evidence could be the client's EU VAT registration number, but if no EU VAT number is provided and the client is in business in the EU, counsel should obtain commercial evidence to this effect. A statement from you that the client is in business would not be sufficient. Where the client belongs outside the EU and Isle of Man, counsel should obtain commercial evidence to confirm the place of belonging. Where no evidence of belonging is obtained, counsel should charge VAT on their services.

EXAMPLE

Assuming the same level of professional charges and counsel's fees as above, your bill should show:

Legal services	£1,200.00	
VAT @ 20%	£240.00	
		£1,440.00
Counsel's fees (including VAT)		£960.00
TOTAL		£2,400.00

If the intention is to take advantage of the concessionary treatment and treat the supply as being made direct to your client, payment of counsel's fees must *not* be made from office account. The option in rule [17.1(b)] of paying into the office account, and then either paying counsel or transferring the amount due to the client account pending payment, cannot therefore be used.

When payment is received from your client, the cheque must either be split as to £1,440 office account and £960 client account, or alternatively the entire sum of [£2,400] must be paid into the client account with a transfer out of the office monies within 14 days of receipt.

6.3 *Tax point for Counsel's fees*

Normally, the tax point for Counsel's services will be determined by payment and not delivery of a fee note. On payment, Counsel's clerk will add the VAT number of Counsel and other particulars required under Regulation 13 of the VAT Regulations 1995 to constitute a document as a VAT invoice so that the receipted fee note is a VAT invoice. This will usually be made out to you/your firm, so that you can claim input tax credit. However, if you alter the fee note so that it is addressed to your client, and input tax credit can be taken by your client, you should keep a photocopy of the VAT invoice, passing the original amended receipted fee note to your client. This is in case the fee note needs to be dealt with on an assessment of costs.[2]

2. You may also find it helpful to refer to the following (see **Part 7** for details): Law Society's Practice Note: VAT on Disbursements, in full (a useful tool for identifying items of expenditure which are classified as disbursements for VAT purposes, and those which are not); Law Society's Practice Note: VAT on Legal Aid Work; and the Bills Guide of the Institute of Legal Finance and Management (ILFM), which provides useful information on the billing concept and process (**www.ilfm.org.uk**).

[5.4] HMRC guidance: Tax on bank and building society interest[1]

S369-S371 Income Tax (Trading and Other Income) Act 2005; S874 Income Tax Act 2007

Bank and building society interest on deposits of clients' money may be held by the solicitor in two types of account. The tax treatment depends on the type of account used, as follows:

1. **Separate designated client account** The client is entitled to the interest arising on the account and depending upon the status of the client the interest may be paid gross or net. The solicitor will simply pass on the interest gross or net to the client.

2. **General client accounts** Deduction of tax does not apply to interest on a general client account.

Where money is deposited into a general client account the interest arises and is chargeable to the solicitor. At the same time, the solicitor owes his or her clients an amount corresponding to the funds deposited, and will account to each client for interest thereon.

Interest paid by the solicitor is taxable on the client as savings income.

The solicitor is to be taxed only on the amount of interest retained in the year (i.e. the difference between the interest received and the interest paid out). Where the amount paid to clients exceeds the interest received, the excess may be allowed as a deduction in computing the profits arising from the profession.

The tax treatment of the interest in the hands of the client is explained at SAIM2000+.

For details of whether the solicitor is obliged to withhold tax on interest paid to clients, see BIM65815.

Note that as the solicitor is a person by or through whom interest is paid, he is a "relevant data holder" for the purposes of Sch23 Finance Act 2011. This means he can be required to produce details of these payments under the data-gathering powers (see BIM65820).

See BIM65830 as regards temporary loans made by solicitors.

1. From Business Income Manual (BIM65805), **www.gov.uk/hmrc-internal-manuals/business-income-manual/bim65805** accessed on 4 November 2016. Please see guidance note (i)(d) to rule 22 of the SRA Accounts Rules 2011.

[6] Compliance

[6.1] Law Society practice note: Compliance officers (extracts)[1]

[Last updated 22 April 2016]

1 Introduction

[…]

1.2 *What's the issue?*

All practices authorised by the Solicitors Regulation Authority (SRA) must appoint a compliance officer for legal practice (COLP) and compliance officer for finance and administration (COFA). Practices authorised by the SRA include recognised bodies (partnerships, LLPs, companies), recognised sole practitioners, and licensed alternative business structures (ABSs).

The SRA Authorisation Rules for Legal Services Bodies and Licensable Bodies outline the requirements for the roles of COLP and COFA.

This practice note explains who can be a COLP and COFA and what these roles entail, as well as recording and reporting requirements.

2 Who can be a COLP or COFA?

[…]

2.2 *Who can be a COFA?*

A COFA must be an individual who:

- is an employee or manager of the practice
- is approved by the SRA for that role
- has consented to undertake the role
- has not been disqualified from acting as a head of finance and administration (HOFA) – as defined in the Legal Services Act 2007
- is of sufficient seniority and in a position of sufficient responsibility to fulfil the role

1. The role of the compliance officer for finance and administration (COFA) is dealt with in rule 6 and guidance note (i) to rule 6 of the SRA Accounts Rules 2011 (see also rule 44, note (iv) and paragraphs 2.1 and 5.4(5) of Appendix 3 to the rules). The following extracts largely concentrate on the COFA's duties: see the full practice note for further detail, including the role of the COLP and the personal liability of compliance officers (COLPs or COFAs). The SRA has also published a statement on compliance officers on its website at **www.sra.org.uk**.

As noted in section 2.1, there is no definition as to what sufficiently senior or responsible might mean.

Unlike a COLP, the COFA does not need to be a lawyer. This allows practices greater flexibility about who they can appoint.

The role relates to the SRA's Accounts Rules.

Therefore the COFA will need a good understanding of the rules applying to solicitors, rather than just a general financial understanding.

[...]

3 The role of compliance officers

[...]

3.2 *The role of the COFA*

The role of the COFA is to:

- take all reasonable steps to ensure compliance with the SRA Accounts Rules
- take all reasonable steps to record failures to comply, in order to be able to recognise material breaches of the SRA Accounts Rules that must be reported to the SRA
- report material failures to comply to the SRA as soon as reasonably practicable. Only ABSs are required to report non-material breaches as part of the Information Report required under Rule 8.7 of the Authorisation Rules (Rule 8 guidance note vii).

In order to be in a position to discharge their role fully, the COFA's must consider whether they:

- have access to all accounting records
- carry out regular checks on the accounting systems
- carry out file and ledger reviews
- ensure that the reporting accountant has prompt access to all the information needed to complete the accountant's report
- take steps to ensure that breaches of the SRA Accounts Rules are remedied promptly
- can report all breaches, which are material either on their own or as part of a pattern, to the SRA and
- can monitor, review and manage risks to compliance with the SRA Accounts Rules.

In order to implement and oversee systems for compliance in relation to the SRA Accounts Rules, the COFA should consider the following:

- a system for ensuring that only the appropriate people authorise payments from client account

- a system for monitoring, reviewing and managing risks
- ensuring that issues of conduct are given appropriate weight in decisions the practice takes, whether on client matters or practice-based issues such as funding
- obtaining the necessary approvals of managers, owners and COLP/COFA
- arrangements to ensure that any duties to clients and others are fully met even when staff are absent.

In addition to the COFA's role in relation to the SRA Accounts Rules, Outcome 10.3 of the SRA Code of Conduct implies that there is a role for COFAs to report to the SRA when the practice is in serious financial difficulties. COFAs therefore also need to consider whether they are able to access information on the practice's overall financial status and be in a position to make an assessment of that status.[2]

3.3 *The role of the COLP and COFA in smaller practices*

The roles of COLP and COFA can be fulfilled by one person and this may be appropriate in smaller practices.

However, those managing smaller practices should also remember that non-lawyers can take on the role of COFA. This provides practices with greater flexibility over who they might appoint, although care should be taken to ensure that those appointed have the relevant experience and knowledge.

The SRA highlights that "what needs to be covered by a practice's compliance plan will depend on factors such as the size and nature of the practice, its work and its areas of risk".

Smaller practices should consider carefully where there are risks to compliance and how these can be mitigated. Systems and processes should be proportionate. Overly complex systems are often by-passed and can become ineffective.

4 The reporting requirements

COLPs and COFAs are required to report material breaches in compliance to the SRA as soon as reasonably practicable. The SRA has indicated that as soon as reasonably practicable in most cases means immediately.

However, as is noted in 3.1 and 3.2 above, ABSs are required to report non-material breaches as part of the Information Report required under Rule 8.7 of the Authorisation Rules (Rule 8 guidance note vii).

2. But see the section on responsibilities in the subsequent SRA statement on COLPS and COFAs, which clarifies that the COFA is not responsible for the systems around sound financial management and that the responsibility for reporting serious financial difficulty lies with the managers and the COLP. It does, however, make the point that due to the close interaction between operating the client account and other financial systems, the COFA should have involvement over the totality of the firm's financial management in order to undertake the role effectively.

4.1 *What is "material"*

When deciding if a breach, or series of breaches are material the COLP or COFA should consider:

- the detriment, or risk of detriment, to clients
- the extent of any risk of loss of confidence in the practice or in the provision of legal services
- the scale of the issue
- the overall impact on the practice, its clients and third parties.

It is important to note that while a single breach may be trivial, if it part of series then it may be material. For this reason, a compliance officer will need systems to identify patterns of breaches.

[...]

4.3 *Keeping records*

COLPs and COFAs should keep a record of breaches in compliance, in order to be able to recognise material failures that must be reported to the SRA. It is for the firm to decide how breaches are recorded and monitored. Practices may consider putting in place a centralised reporting system to allow them to capture and record breaches in compliance.

While data on all breaches may be difficult to collect, particularly in larger organisations, it can be valuable. The data may highlight areas where the risk of non-compliance is higher and allow the practice to put in place measures to mitigate against the risk of further non-compliance. The data can also be used to measure the effectiveness of interventions to improve compliance.

It is also important that the data is captured in such a way that the COLPs and COFAs can identify any patterns of breaches which may be material and must be reported to the SRA. This will be easier in smaller practices, where there are likely to be fewer breaches reported.

5 Contingency planning

The SRA guidance highlights the need to have in place arrangements to ensure that any duties to clients and others are fully met even when staff are absent. As with all areas of the business practices should give consideration to how they will manage the absence of a compliance officer (e.g. due to holiday or illness, or retirement).

If the practice ceases to have a compliance officer it will need to:

- inform the SRA,
- designate another manager or employee to replace its previous compliance officer and
- make an application to the SRA for temporary approval of the new COLP or COFA, as appropriate.

This should be done immediately or in any event within seven days. Where a compliance officer is likely to be absent for a significant length of time they may need to be replaced. The practice should discuss whether replacement is appropriate action with their supervision team at the SRA.

6 Your personal liability

As noted in section 3 above, the SRA has made statements to the effect that COLPs and COFAs will not be used as "sacrificial lambs" where there is a lack of a firm-wide compliance.

Rather, the SRA sees compliance officers as the formal points of contact for compliance in a practice. While the managers of a practice continue to bear the ultimate responsibility for a practice's compliance, compliance officers may also face regulatory action personally where they fail to meet their responsibilities.

For this reason, it is important that compliance officers consider their personal liability and are satisfied that appropriate safeguards are in place. It is for individual compliance officers to reach an agreement with their practice as to the best way to protect against any potential liability.

There are a number of potential options that you may want to consider, including:

- an indemnity agreement
- an amendment to your employment contract
- an endorsement on the practice's professional indemnity insurance (PII) policy, or
- an insurance product (e.g. Directors' and Officers' (D&O) cover or a specific COLP/COFA product).

[...]

[6.2] SRA case study: Recording and reporting breaches (extracts)

[Last updated April 2014]

You need to have a system in place to record any failures in compliance so that you can monitor overall compliance with the firm's obligations and assess the effectiveness of its arrangements and systems. The record of breaches also allows you, in your compliance officer role, to decide whether you need to report breaches as material, because they form a pattern of non-compliance. Breaches which are material – either in themselves or because of a pattern – must be reported to the SRA as soon as reasonably practical. In most cases, that should mean immediately.

A common question from compliance officers is what constitutes a material breach. In considering whether a failure or breach is material, you will need to take account of various factors such as:

- the detriment, or risk of detriment, to clients;
- the risk of loss of confidence in the firm or in the provision of legal services;
- the scale of the issue; and
- the overall impact on the practice, clients and third parties.

Below are some examples of recent reports the SRA has received from compliance officers.

[...]

Report 3

The firm's COFA reported a number of SRA Accounts Rules breaches arising from four matters dealt with in the probate department.

Estate A

In December 2013 the firm transferred the costs of £1,551 from client to office account, without sending a copy of the invoice or other written notification of costs to the client, namely the Executor of the estate. The breach was identified by the COFA on 10 January. The next day a copy invoice and apology was sent to the client.

Client B

The firm transferred the sum of £280 from the wrong client ledger. Instead of taking payment from Mr B's ledger for drawing up a will, payment was taken from the ledger for Mrs B's estate, of which Mr B was the executor. The breach was identified on 29 January – by 3 February, the funds had been transferred back to the correct ledger, a new bill delivered to Mr B with notification of the breach, and funds appropriately transferred from his ledger.

Estate C

In October 2013 a review of client balances identified that the firm still held £3,881 for the estate although final distribution had occurred earlier in the year. Once identified, steps were immediately taken to re-establish contact with the residuary beneficiary and the balance was discharged, with a sum in lieu of interest.

It is arguable that none of the above breaches, in isolation, is material. The nature of the breaches meant that there was minimal risk to clients/client money and the duration was short with immediate action being taken to rectify the breaches once identified. Factors that would make the individual breaches material might include:

- larger sums of money being involved;
- actual detriment to clients;
- longer delays in either the breaches being identified or being rectified.

However, taken as a pattern, the breaches are material. They all arise from work undertaken in the probate department, and with three different breaches occurring over a short period of time, it suggests a lack of awareness and compliance with the SRA Accounts Rules, particularly in probate matters.

Estate D

The report also identified breaches arising in Estate D, where the solicitor was the sole executor of the estate. Over a period of two years, the Head of the Probate department had transferred monies from client to office account for payment of costs on six occasions, totalling £36,956. There were no invoices on the matter, and at no point were the beneficiaries notified of costs, even though they greatly exceeded the original estimate of £12,000, which included a percentage element based on value of the estate.

In itself, this breach is material. There is a pattern of repeated breaches over a long period of time and a significant detriment to the client. The will provided for a number of legacies, but with the remainder of the estate being left to two residuary beneficiaries. The costs are significant and impact on the residue of the estate. However, the beneficiaries had not had an opportunity to challenge costs because they were unaware of the position.

The COFA reported the above matters to the SRA. All matters have been rectified and the firm has put in place a range of measures to address the issues. This has included a full audit of costs and client money transfers in the probate department, significant training on client care and accounts issues for that team and wider training across the firm. The COFA has also implemented additional safeguards in the accounts team and a system of spot checks on files.

[6.3] SRA case study: When is a breach "material" or "non-material"? (extracts)

[Last updated May 2013]

A common dilemma facing COLPs and COFAs is whether or not a breach is material and therefore needs to be reported to the SRA.

These scenarios are examples of reports[1] we have recently received. We outline the factors that COLPs and COFAs should take into consideration in reaching a decision on whether the breach is material or non-material.

Scenario 2

Details of the report

The firm's COFA reported that their bank had incorrectly debited £28.69 from their client account, instead of the office account, to pay for the firm's telephone messaging service. The error was identified the following day and rectified immediately.

Is it a breach?

Client money may only be withdrawn from client account in accordance with rule 20.1 of the SRA Accounts Rules 2011, for example when it is properly required to make payment on behalf of a client. The use of client money to pay the firm's telephone messaging service was a breach of rule 20.1 and so should be recorded as such by the COFA.

Is the breach material?

Although client money was incorrectly used, this arose as a result of a bank error. The firm's accounting systems meant that it was identified the next day and immediately rectified by them. The overall impact meant that it was a **non-material breach** which did not need reporting to the SRA.

Additional issues to consider

It appears that the systems for ensuring compliance with the rules were operating effectively, and the breach arose as a result of a bank error. So the COFA may wish to consider contacting the bank to flag the issue and reminding them of the requirements relating to the operation of client and office accounts.

1. Two reports from COFAs included in the case study are reproduced here.

Scenario 3

Details of the report

The firm's COFA made a report of a number of instances of non-compliance with rule 20 of the SRA Accounts Rules 2011. Payments which should have been made from the office account were incorrectly made out of client account, as follows:

Date of payment	Amount of payment	Date identified	Date rectified
30 January	£22	5 February	8 February
5 February	£6	14 February	15 February
18 February	£76	20 February	22 February
11 March	£105	14 March	18 March
28 March	£22	3 April	4 April
8 April	£18	11 April	16 April

Four of the six payments were bank charges (e.g. for international transfers), but two related to payments requested by the fee earner for disbursements where funds had not been received from the client for those.

Is it a breach?

Each client's money must only be used for that client's matters. This was not the case with the six payments. The use of the client account money was not in accordance with rule 20.1 of the SRA Accounts Rules 2011 and was a breach that should be recorded.

Is the breach material?

The first issue to consider is the risk to client's monies. Individually, none of the payments was a significant amount but in each case client money was being used inappropriately and there was a pattern of breaches over an extended period of time.

The firm's accounting systems meant that there was a delay in identifying the breaches and in two instances, a failure in the firm's internal controls allowed the payments to be made incorrectly from the client account. Once identified, the breach was not rectified immediately in any of the cases despite the requirement to repay any money improperly withdrawn from client account promptly, as soon as it is discovered.

The failings in the accounting systems and the pattern of breaches, although small amounts, meant that the breach was material.

Additional issues to consider

The COFA will need to review their accounting systems and records, as well as internal controls regarding payments from the client account, to ensure compliance. They will also need to identify the issues with the bank in relation to bank charges needing to be paid from the office account.

[6.4] SRA Ethics guidance: Accountant's report (AR1) and guidance for firms and accountants[1]

[Last updated on 24 June 2016]

Due to a change on 1 November 2015 you need to determine which version of our rules apply to you in relation to the reporting account requirements.

If your next accounting period end date is **before 1 November 2015**, you will need to

1. comply with version 14 of the SRA Accounts Rules 2011, and

2. use the accountant's report form (AR1) at Appendix 5 of version 14 of the rules and the reporting accountant's checklist at Appendix 4 of the same rules,

The guidance below will not apply to your firm.

If your next accounting period end date is on **or after 1 November 2015**, you will need to

1. comply with version 15 of the SRA Accounts Rules 2011,

2. use the new AR1 – Accountant's report form (PDF 3 pages, 258K) and the guidance on completing the form below,

3. check if the exemptions set out in Rule 32A.1A of the SRA Accounts Rules apply.

1. Version 15 of the SRA Handbook introduced a new form of accountant's report (AR1) for use by all firms with an accounting period ending on or after 1 November 2015. This annex contains the SRA's guidance on completing the form of report (see **www.sra.org.uk** for future updates).

Version 15 of the SRA Accounts Rules 2011, set out in **Part 1** of this Manual, includes an exemption from the requirement to obtain an accountant's report based on the amount of client money held, in addition to the exemption where only Legal Aid Agency money is held (guidance on the exemptions is also included in this annex). Reporting accountants no longer carry out a prescribed set of test procedures or complete a prescribed checklist, using their professional judgement in preparing the report.

Although the guidance on completing AR1 does not form part of the SRA Handbook, a firm's managers and compliance officer for finance and administration should read it carefully, as well as the reporting accountant, as the SRA may take it into account when exercising its regulatory functions.

Transitional arrangements mean that firms with an accounting period end date before 1 November 2015 must continue to comply with the requirements for accountants' reports in version 14 of the SRA Accounts Rules 2011 (see **www.sra.org.uk**). The reporting accountant will use the reporting accountant's checklist at Appendix 4, and the form of report at Appendix 5, of that version of the rules.

Accountants' Reports for overseas practice (AR2)

If your next accounting period end date is **before 1 November 2015**, you are still required to obtain and deliver an accountant's report, regardless of its qualification. This should be delivered to us within six months of the period end date. This also applies to final accountants reports. You will need to

1. comply with version 14 of the SRA Accounts Rules 2011, and

2. use the accountant's report form (AR2)

In all dealings with client money (overseas), you must ensure compliance with Rule 2C.1 of the SRA Overseas Rules 2013.

If your next accounting period end date is **on or after 1 November 2015**, our rules do not require you to obtain or deliver an accountant's report. This also applies to final accountants reports.

However, you should be aware that we may require you to deliver an accountant's report.

GUIDANCE ON COMPLETING THE NEW ANNUAL ACCOUNTANT'S REPORT (AR1 FORM)

Please note: This guidance is applicable if your next accounting period end date is **on or after 1 November 2015.**

Status

Whilst this document does not form part of the SRA Handbook, the SRA may have regard to it when exercising its regulatory functions. We expect both firms and the reporting accountant to have read it carefully prior to commencing their programme of work.

Purpose of this guidance

This guidance is intended to assist reporting accountants in completing the report. It will also be of interest to the firm's Compliance Officer for Finance and Administration (COFA) and managers in their discussions with the reporting accountant.

Introduction

We require firms to obtain an independent accountant's report to confirm that the overarching objective to keep client money safe is met. Rule 1.2 of the SRA Accounts Rules 2011 (the Account Rules) sets out in more detail the key obligations that firms must meet to demonstrate that client money is safe, including the delivery of an annual accountant's reports.

We have modified our approach to the provision of accountant's reports. We expect reporting accountants to exercise their professional judgement when preparing and finalising the report and to require only qualified reports to be submitted to us. This guidance is intended to assist accountants in completing the report.

If during an accounting period, firms have met certain criteria around

(i) the small amounts of client money held (an average of less than or equal to £10,000 as well as a maximum of less than or equal to £250,000) at each reconciliation date or

(ii) the holding or receipt of money only from the Legal Aid Agency,

they may be exempted from the requirement to obtain an accountant's report; for further detail, see Rule 32.

Rule 39 of the Accounts Rules, which required accountants to undertake a lengthy standard number of detailed checks and tests when examining a firm's accounting records, has now been removed. Instead, Rule [43A.1] requires the accountants to use their professional judgement in assessing a firm's compliance and deciding whether their subsequent report needs to be qualified.

In our view, the report should only be qualified where the breaches identified are material and where client money is at risk. (See section 2 and 3 below for examples.). Material breaches are likely to arise as a result of an intention to break the rules and/or as a result of a significant weakness in the firm's systems and controls which should be in place to prevent breaches. Breaches arising from administrative errors are less likely to be material, but still could be if they are persistent, derive from a lack of controls or break down of controls, and have put client money at risk. We recognise that trivial, non-material breaches of the Accounts Rules do occur in many firms and we are not expecting all identified breaches to be notified to us in the form of a qualified report.

In all cases, the reporting accountant should ensure the work they undertake is proportionate and targeted to the size of firm and nature of the work the firm undertakes.

We accept that in light of the current prescriptive nature of the Accounts Rules, both the accountants and the firms which instruct them may need some assistance and guidance at this time in

- planning what work might need to be undertaken and how to assure that client money is properly safeguarded; and
- assessing what factors might lead to the accountant to decide that the report should be qualified and therefore submitted by the firm to us for further consideration of the risks posed.

We will keep this guidance under review and update it, as necessary.

Please note that we have also issued separate guidance on accounting procedures and systems that reporting accountants and firms will wish to have regard to – see SRA Guidelines – Accounting procedures and Systems [SRA Accounts Rules 2011, Appendix 3].

Some firms may wish to ask their reporting accountants to undertake additional work around the firm's systems and controls to aid the development of best practice, around compliance issues such as the effective operation of office account, the firm's compliance with the "client due diligence' requirements of the Money Laundering Regulations and cyber security. Ultimately it will be a matter for the firm to consider what support it may need.

This Guidance is designed to set out the areas of work that a reporting accountant may wish to consider to enable the completion of the accountant's report and the reporting of appropriate concerns to us. Our aim is to ensure that consumers, SRA-authorised firms and the SRA has an appropriate level of assurance that there are adequate controls over client money while not inflating inappropriately the cost to firms, and ultimately to consumers, by any unnecessary mandatory procedures.

Reporting accountants are under a duty pursuant to Section 34(9) of the Solicitors Act 1974 and the terms of their engagement with SRA-authorised firms to immediately report to us any evidence of theft or fraud or significant concerns about the fitness and propriety of the firm to hold client money (see also Rule 35.1 of the Accounts Rules). The duty also extends to reporting to us a termination of the accountant's appointment based on their intention to issue a qualified accountant's report. If the reporting accountant considers that their work has been limited in scope to the extent that they feel unable to make the declarations required on the accountant's report form, then they should qualify the report on that basis and make a report to us. We have recently extended the obligation to also inform us immediately if the reporting accountants discover a failure by the firm to submit a previously qualified accountant's report to us as required by the Accounts Rules (see Rule 32).

About this guidance

This guidance has three sections:

- the provisions of the Accounts Rules that need to be considered by the reporting accountant and which need to be covered by the accountant's report
- the sorts of factors that may lead to notification of issues and result in the submission of a qualified accountant's report
- a table setting out some examples of the types of checks or test procedures that may be undertaken by the reporting accountant and guidance about the types of results/situations the accountants and the firm's COFA and managers may expect to see in various/different firms.

Section 1

We only require reporting accountants to assess compliance with certain elements of the Accounts Rules. These provisions are set out below:

- Rule 1 – The overarching objective and underlying principles
- Rule 7 – Duty to remedy breaches
- Rule 13 – Client accounts
- Rule 14 – Uses of a client account
- Rule 17 – Receipt and transfer of costs
- Rule 18 – Receipt of mixed payments
- Rule 20 – Withdrawals from a client account
- Rule 21 – Method of and authority for withdrawal from a client account

- Rule 27 – Restrictions on transfers between clients
- Rule 29 – Accounting records for client accounts.

However, if the circumstances outlined in Rule(s) 8, 9, 10,15, 16 and 19 are applicable the accountant is required to assess compliance accordingly.

Section 2

In our view the intention to rely on the reporting accountants' professional judgement means that we do not consider it appropriate to define when a report must be qualified. The assessment requires an understanding of the seriousness of all the risks posed in the context of the firm's size and complexity, areas of work, systems and controls and compliance history. However, there are some areas where both our and the reporting accountants' experiences shows a risk to client money and which we would therefore expect may lead the reporting accountant to consider a qualification. Notwithstanding these matters, if the reporting accountant identifies a matter that they consider should be drawn to the attention of the SRA, the report should be qualified and submitted to us. SRA-authorised firms should not seek to prevent a reporting accountant from qualifying a report on the basis that the qualification does not fall into the factors set out below.

These factors (which are illustrative only and not intended to be exhaustive) include:

Serious factors – the presence of one or more is likely to be material and/or represent a significant weakness in the firm's system and controls, and lead towards a definite qualification:

- A significant and/or unreplaced shortfall (including client debit balances or office credit balances) on client account, including client monies held elsewhere unless caused by bank error and rectified in a timely manner (see sections 3.1, 3.2 below).
- Evidence of the wilful disregard for the safety of client money and assets and deliberate non-compliance with the Accounts Rules and/or Accounting Guidelines
- Actual or suspected fraud or dishonesty by the managers or employees of the firm (that may impact upon the safety of client money).
- Situation where material breaches that have not been reported by the firm to us in accordance with the Authorisation Rules or the separate duty to report a serious failure to comply with the rules in the SRA's Handbook or serious misconduct by any person in accordance with Outcome 10.3 and 10.4 of the SRA Code of Conduct 2011. This is in respect of material breaches that the accountant becomes aware of as a result of work undertaken in respect of client money. A detailed assessment of the firm's financial position is not required.
- No or wholly inadequate accounting records or records not retained (Rule 29.17).
- A failure to provide documentation requested by the reporting accountant.
- Three way client account bank reconciliations not carried out (Rule 29.12).
- Where the client account used as a banking facility (Rule 14.5) or where there is actual or suspected fraud or dishonesty by the firm.

Moderate factors – the presence of which one or more may be material and/or represent a significant weakness in the firm's systems and controls, and lead towards a potential qualification:

- A significant, fully replaced shortfall (including client debit balances or office credit balances) on client account, including client monies held elsewhere unless caused by bank error and rectified in a timely manner (see sections 3.1, 3.2 below).
- Actual or suspected fraud or dishonesty by third parties that may impact on the safety of client funds.
- Material breaches that have not been reported to us within one month of identification.
- Accounting records insufficient or unreliable (Section 3.7 below) or not retained for 6 years (Rule 29.17).
- Three way client account bank reconciliations not regularly carried out at least every 5 weeks (Rule 29.12).
- Poor control environment (Sections 3.3, 3.4, 3.5, 3.6 below).
- Performance or review of three way bank reconciliations not adequate (Section 3.7 below).
- Longstanding residual balances due to clients (Section 3.8 below).
- Improper use of suspense accounts (Section 3.9 below).

Section 3

The purpose of this section is not to provide a definitive list of all test procedures required to be performed by the reporting accountants. The aim is to provide some examples of the sorts of areas of work that might be used by the reporting accountants to test compliance with the relevant Accounts Rules as set out in Section 1.

Appropriate planning by the accountant may mean that testing in one area may cover issues of compliance in other areas. For example, by checking the client account bank reconciliation it may be possible to be satisfied that a number of the key rules are being complied with. Again the examples are not mandatory and are intended to be helpful to both the accountants and the firms concerned.

In all cases, we suggest that the reporting accountants discusses with the firm the areas that they intend to cover in their work programme. It is, however, the accountants' responsibility to ensure that the work they undertake is sufficient to enable completion of the accountants' report and proportionate and targeted to the size of firm and nature of its work.

The section also includes some guidance on what processes and procedures the reporting accountant may expect to see in an above adequate, adequate and below adequate firm. These are included to assist both the reporting accountant and the firm's COFA and managers responsible for compliance with the Rules by indicating what good, average and poor looks like. However, we would only expect firms in the below adequate section to lead to the issue of a qualified report and if the factors set out in Section 2 above are present.

TABLE

Outcome of Reporting Accountant test procedures	General guidance	Examples of areas of focus (work should be proportionate, not all of these will always be relevant. Accountants should use their judgement in performing suitable work. Checking compliance with the Rules may be achieved by carrying out a selection of tests)	Guidance – indicative of firm with above adequate processes and procedures	Guidance – indicative of a firm with adequate processes and controls	Guidance – indicative of a firm with below adequate processes and controls that may lead to a qualification
3.1 Client money in client account Have you seen any evidence of the placing of client money in any account or location other than a client bank account, or any delay in the placing of money into a client bank account, for a period of time that has resulted in a loss to a client or would otherwise give you concerns about potential fraud or losses to client money?	A delay of 5 working days over that required by the rules is considered likely to result in a loss to the client or is evidence of a lack of attention or focus on the rules, which require client money to be banked 'without delay' or to be transferred within 2 or 14 days.	• Testing of office account receipts (to assess if receipts include client money). • Testing whether client money identified in the office account was transferred in accordance with the rules.	No incidents noted of client money being placed in any account or location other than a client bank account.	Minimal incidents of client money being placed in any account or location other than a client bank account. In such incidents, the law firm rectified the issue promptly (within 5 working days), transferring client money to an appropriate client bank account.	• Client money was routinely placed in an account or location other than a client bank account and/or there were delays of over 5 working days above that required by the rules in transferring these funds to a client account.

Outcome of Reporting Accountant test procedures	General guidance	Examples of areas of focus	Guidance – indicative of firm with above adequate processes and procedures	Guidance – indicative of a firm with adequate processes and controls	Guidance – indicative of a firm with below adequate processes and controls that may lead to a qualification
Have you seen any round sum transfers between the client account and the office account? *Rule 7, Rule 13, Rule 14, Rule 17, Rule 18*	Round sum transfers between the client account and the office account may be indicative of client monies being improperly used to finance business operations.	• Testing whether client money received was banked in accordance with the rules. • Testing office account to client account transfers to identify number and reasons for such transfers.	No incidents noted of delays in placing client money into a client bank account (these include money in an office account that becomes client money through, for example, overpayments, credit notes issued to clients in respect of paid bills and cancelled cheques on disbursements).	No incidents noted of banking client money into a client bank account with a delay of in excess of 5 working days (these include money in an office account that becomes client money through, for example, overpayments, credit notes issued to clients in respect of paid bills and cancelled cheques on disbursements).	• Incidents were noted of a delay in excess of 5 working days in banking of client money into a client bank account (these include money in office account that becomes client money through, for example, overpayments, credit notes issued to clients in respect of paid bills and cancelled cheques on disbursements).

Outcome of Reporting Accountant test procedures	**General guidance**	**Examples of areas of focus**	**Guidance – indicative of firm with above adequate processes and procedures**	**Guidance – indicative of a firm with adequate processes and controls**	**Guidance – indicative of a firm with below adequate processes and controls that may lead to a qualification**
		• Testing client bank reconciliation (for example, to assess if reconciling items lead to banking of client money outside the timeframes in the rules or to identify round sum transfers in breach of the Rules).	No incidents noted of transfers between client accounts and the office account that were not within the Rules and appropriately authorised.	No incidents noted of transfers between client accounts and the office account that were not within the Rules and appropriately authorised.	• Round sum amounts were transferred out of client account without both authorisation and proper reason (for example, payment of a bill or a disbursement).

Outcome of Reporting Accountant test procedures	General guidance	Examples of areas of focus	Guidance – indicative of firm with above adequate processes and procedures	Guidance – indicative of a firm with adequate processes and controls	Guidance – indicative of a firm with below adequate processes and controls that may lead to a qualification
		• Testing office bank reconciliations (for example, to assess if reconciling items lead to banking of client money in the office account or to identify round sum transfers not required).			

Outcome of Reporting Accountant test procedures	General guidance	Examples of areas of focus	Guidance – indicative of firm with above adequate processes and procedures	Guidance – indicative of a firm with adequate processes and controls	Guidance – indicative of a firm with below adequate processes and controls that may lead to a qualification
3.2 Overdrawn client/credit office ledgers – shortages Have you identified any debit balances on client ledgers, or credit balances on the office ledger, for a period of greater than 14 days that indicate: • the firm has used other clients' money on client matters; • client money has not promptly been placed in a client account; or • client money being inappropriately withdrawn from client account.	Law firms should have controls to avoid client debit balances arising and that prompt a regular review and investigation of office credit balances.	• Test the computerised system to assess if debit balances can be created (for example, by processing a payment in excess of the balance held on client account in respect of a particular client).	Systems and practices are such that debit balances do not arise. A listing of credit balances on the office ledgers is reviewed at least weekly and each credit balance is investigated, fully understood and action taken where necessary to remove client funds in office account.	Debit balances on client ledgers are reviewed at least weekly and necessary action taken to remove the debit balance. A listing of credit balances on the office ledger is reviewed at least monthly and each credit balance is investigated, fully understood and action taken where necessary to remove client funds in office account.	• There are no processes in place that would routinely identify debit balances on client ledgers. • Debit balances that are identified through ad-hoc procedures are reviewed but either no action is taken to investigate and properly remove the debit balance or such action is not undertaken for over a month from the date of identification.

Outcome of Reporting Accountant test procedures	General guidance	Examples of areas of focus	Guidance – indicative of firm with above adequate processes and procedures	Guidance – indicative of a firm with adequate processes and controls	Guidance – indicative of a firm with below adequate processes and controls that may lead to a qualification
Rule 7, Rule 13, Rule 14, Rule 17, Rule 18, Rule 20, Rule 21, Rule 27, SRA Guideline 2.7 and 4.5		• Where debit balances can be processed, test debit balances that arose throughout the period and assess the timeframe taken to remove the debit balance – also understand why the debit balance arose.			• There are no processes in place to identify credit balances on the office ledger. • Office credit balances that are identified through ad-hoc procedures are reviewed but either no action is taken to investigate and properly remove the credit balance or such action is not undertaken for over a month from the date of identification.

Outcome of Reporting Accountant test procedures	General guidance	Examples of areas of focus	Guidance – indicative of firm with above adequate processes and procedures	Guidance – indicative of a firm with adequate processes and controls	Guidance – indicative of a firm with below adequate processes and controls that may lead to a qualification
3.3 Withdrawals from client account Are withdrawals of client money made only in accordance with pre-approved authorisation procedures? *Rule 20, SRA Guideline 4.1*	It is important to check if payment withdrawals are made in accordance with authorisation procedures.	• Test documentation that supports regular review of office credit balances and check that action is taken to remove necessary office credit balances within one month of the date on which it was identified. • Test office credit balances arising in the year to assess if any indicate that client money was in office account for an inappropriate length of time.	A formal client account withdrawals process is fully documented and adhered to. Withdrawals can only be processed once the proper authorisation has been obtained. Where electronic authorities are permitted, these are only made with a secure IT approval process (note: email approval is not considered secure).	A client account withdrawals process exists and is adhered to, but is not formally documented. Withdrawals can only be processed once the proper authorisation has been obtained.	• A client account withdrawals process does not exist. • A client account withdrawals process exists but is not adhered to. • Unauthorised withdrawals from client bank account have been identified.

Outcome of Reporting Accountant test procedures	General guidance	Examples of areas of focus	Guidance – indicative of firm with above adequate processes and procedures	Guidance – indicative of a firm with adequate processes and controls	Guidance – indicative of a firm with below adequate processes and controls that may lead to a qualification
3.4 Control systems Can the firm demonstrate that it has effective processes (both manual and IT) that are designed to ensure the integrity (i.e. working order) and security (access) over client accounting records and money? *Rule 29, SRA Guideline 5.5*	Effective IT systems may include – access controls, firewalls, software and hardware maintenance contracts. Effective manual systems may include – a system of operating controls to prevent misuse of client money and monitoring controls that would identify such misuse.	• Test a sample of client account withdrawals to assess if appropriate client account withdrawals authorisations were in place at the time of the withdrawal. • Consider whether unauthorised withdrawals could be indicative of fraud/dishonesty • Obtain documentation about how the firm controls their IT environment.	A strong control environment exists which includes the following: • The client accounting system is fully documented and includes notes over billing, payments, transfers, new client take on, etc. • Password access to the IT system/s and passwords are changed at least quarterly.	A reasonable IT control environment exists which includes the following: • Password access to the IT system/s and passwords are changed at least annually. • IT user access controls are in place. • Program changes to the IT system are always fully documented and approved before changes commence.	• The control environment does not include characteristics of the "adequate process and controls" noted opposite (*Note: the controls should be commensurate to the size and complexity of the law firm*). • The accountant has identified, through their work, a control environment that is ineffective or not fit for purpose.

Outcome of Reporting Accountant test procedures	General guidance	Examples of areas of focus	Guidance – indicative of firm with above adequate processes and procedures	Guidance – indicative of a firm with adequate processes and controls	Guidance – indicative of a firm with below adequate processes and controls that may lead to a qualification
		• Ask the firm to demonstrate either by providing you with a copy of their, or by showing you, their IT access controls. • Accountants are not expected to perform extensive work around the IT or manual control environment at the firm. But rather are expected to report any results based on the work that they *have* done	• IT user access controls are in place. • Program changes to the IT system are always fully documented and approved before changes commence. • Leavers ID's and passwords are immediately removed from the IT system once they have left the law firm.	• Leavers ID's and passwords are removed from the IT system within one month of the individual leaving the law firm. • Firewalls are in place. • IT general controls are documented to a standard that is commensurate with the size and complexity of the business.	

Outcome of Reporting Accountant test procedures	General guidance	Examples of areas of focus	Guidance – indicative of firm with above adequate processes and procedures	Guidance – indicative of a firm with adequate processes and controls	Guidance – indicative of a firm with below adequate processes and controls that may lead to a qualification
			• Firewalls are in place. • IT general controls are documented to a standard that is commensurate with the size and complexity of the business.	• The client accounting system is not fully documented, but notes exist which support the necessary cycles, e.g. billing, payments, transfers, new client take on, etc.	

Outcome of Reporting Accountant test procedures	General guidance	Examples of areas of focus	Guidance – indicative of firm with above adequate processes and procedures	Guidance – indicative of a firm with adequate processes and controls	Guidance – indicative of a firm with below adequate processes and controls that may lead to a qualification
3.5 General control environment Have you seen any evidence where the systems have not operated effectively or where the firm has not been able to properly account to clients for client money held? *Rule 7, Rule 13, Rule 14, Rule 17, Rule 18, Rule 29, SRA Guidelines*	The COFA or a member of the finance team should (reporting results to the firm's managers) regularly review systems and processes and ensures they are fit for purpose in accordance with the requirements of the Rules. Reporting structures within the firm should be such that accounts staff readily report errors and systems weaknesses to the COFA.	• Consider the firm's breaches register, the extent to which breaches are recorded, followed up. Reviewed, action taken. • Consider previous Accountant's reports. • Consider previous years' Accountant's reports and matters reported in those, where appropriate.	The COFA or a member of the finance team reviews the systems and processes at least annually and implements actions for improvement where appropriate. The COFA ensures action is taken for all issues included in the Accountant's Report (and any subsequent or additional work commissioned by the firm	The COFA, a member of the finance team or the Internal Audit team reviews the systems and processes every two to three years and implements actions for improvement where appropriate.	• There is no formal review of the systems and processes. • No action is taken from the findings included in the Accountant's Report or any separate report issued to management. • Also see points under 3.7 below.

Outcome of Reporting Accountant test procedures	General guidance	Examples of areas of focus	Guidance – indicative of firm with above adequate processes and procedures	Guidance – indicative of a firm with adequate processes and controls	Guidance – indicative of a firm with below adequate processes and controls that may lead to a qualification
		• Internal audit • Complaints by clients? • Review list of non-moving client account balances	Also see points under 3.7 below.	The COFA ensures action is taken for all issues included in the Accountant's Report (and any subsequent or additional work commissioned by the firm Also see points under 3.7 below.	

Outcome of Reporting Accountant test procedures	General guidance	Examples of areas of focus	Guidance – indicative of firm with above adequate processes and procedures	Guidance – indicative of a firm with adequate processes and controls	Guidance – indicative of a firm with below adequate processes and controls that may lead to a qualification
3.6 General Compliance with the Rules Have you seen evidence of management review/controls designed to ensure compliance with the SRA Accounts Rules? *SRA Guidelines*	Firms are required to undertake three way reconciliations between the bank, cash book and client ledger listings at least every 5 weeks. There should be an evidenced, timely review of such reconciliations. Recommended processes would include regular staff (finance **and** legal professionals) training, breach log review, exception reports.	• Testing of client bank account reconciliations, office bank account reconciliations, the three way reconciliation of the cash book, client ledger listing and bank accounts and the breach register (to assess if they have been reviewed by at least the COFA or another appropriate individual).	The COFA, or another appropriate individual within the firm, performs a review on more than one occasion each month, of SRA Accounts Rules compliance, including a review of (i) client bank account reconciliations, (ii) office bank account reconciliations, (iii) three way reconciliation of the cash book, client ledger listing and bank accounts; and (iv) breach register.	The COFA, or another appropriate individual within the firm, performs at least a five-weekly review of SRA Accounts Rules compliance, including a review of (i) client bank account reconciliation, (ii) office bank account reconciliations, (iii) three way reconciliation of the cash book, client ledger listing and bank accounts; and (iv) breach register.	• No or insufficiently frequent bank reconciliations are undertaken • There is no review of one or more of the bank reconciliations or the breaches register.

Outcome of Reporting Accountant test procedures	General guidance	Examples of areas of focus	Guidance – indicative of firm with above adequate processes and procedures	Guidance – indicative of a firm with adequate processes and controls	Guidance – indicative of a firm with below adequate processes and controls that may lead to a qualification
		• Where reconciling items appear on two consecutive monthly reconciliations, check that that they have been identified, challenged and appropriate steps have been taken to remove them. • Review of documentation supporting reviews performed by the COFA over the client money control environment.	Evidence exists of challenge by the COFA and actions taken to improve the control environment. The COFA, or another appropriate individual within the firm, performs a review annually, or as appropriate, of the client money control environment and, where appropriate, takes action to improve processes.	Challenge by the COFA happens, but no evidence exists to support this. The COFA, or another appropriate individual within the firm, performs a review annually, or as appropriate, of the client money control environment and, where appropriate, takes action to improve processes.	• The COFA, or another appropriate individual within the firm, performs ad-hoc and/or informal review of SRA Accounts Rules compliance, including a review of (i) client bank account reconciliation, (ii) office bank account reconciliations, (iii) three way reconciliation of the cash book, client ledger listing and bank accounts; and

Outcome of Reporting Accountant test procedures	General guidance	Examples of areas of focus	Guidance – indicative of firm with above adequate processes and procedures	Guidance – indicative of a firm with adequate processes and controls	Guidance – indicative of a firm with below adequate processes and controls that may lead to a qualification
			The COFA, or another appropriate individual within the firm, performs a detailed annual review of the training requirements for staff – both finance and legal professionals and ensures appropriate training is delivered to these individuals.	The COFA, or another appropriate individual within the firm, performs a detailed annual review of the training requirements for staff – both finance and legal professionals and ensure appropriate training is delivered to these individuals.	(iv) breach register. No challenge or action is taken by the COFA. ● The same reconciling item (other than un-presented cheques) appears on two consecutive monthly bank reconciliations without clear evidence that it has been challenged by the COFA

Outcome of Reporting Accountant test procedures	General guidance	Examples of areas of focus	Guidance – indicative of firm with above adequate processes and procedures	Guidance – indicative of a firm with adequate processes and controls	Guidance – indicative of a firm with below adequate processes and controls that may lead to a qualification
			If it is not the COFA who performs these tasks, there should be evidence of reporting to and review by the COFA.	If it is not the COFA who performs these tasks, there should be evidence of reporting to and review by the COFA.	• The COFA, or another appropriate individual within the firm, does not perform an ad-hoc review at least annually of the client money control environment or does not take action, where appropriate, to improve processes. If it is not the COFA who performs these tasks, there is no evidence of reporting to and review by the COFA.

Outcome of Reporting Accountant test procedures	General guidance	Examples of areas of focus	Guidance – indicative of firm with above adequate processes and procedures	Guidance – indicative of a firm with adequate processes and controls	Guidance – indicative of a firm with below adequate processes and controls that may lead to a qualification
3.7 Accounting records Does the firm operate a system that allows accounting records to be maintained in an up-to date manner and in compliance with the Rules *Rule 29, SRA Guideline 2.3*	Processes in place are designed to ensure between daily and weekly postings of transactions (depending on size of firm). Exceptions may arise due to circumstances where transactions are outside the ordinary course of business – evidence should exist of law firm's timely investigation and follow up of such items.	• Testing of client account receipts, payments, transfers. • Testing of office account receipts, payments and transfers. In all cases, this would be to assess if accounting records have been kept up to date under the appropriate timeframes. • Consider if the firm is able to, quickly and easily, account to clients for money held on their behalf.	All client and office transactions are posted to the accounting system by the end of the next working day. The law firm would, at all times, be able to account to clients for client money held.	All client and office transactions are accounted for, either in the system or through an alternative system (e.g. through use of spreadsheet before batch processing in the system) by 5 working days following the transaction. The law firm would be able to account to clients for client money held.	• Client and office account transactions are routinely posted to the client account system in excess of 5 working days after the date of the transaction. • The firm does not have an accounting system that is commensurate with the size and complexity of the business and, as a consequence, cannot account to clients accurately for monies held.

Outcome of Reporting Accountant test procedures	General guidance	Examples of areas of focus	Guidance – indicative of firm with above adequate processes and procedures	Guidance – indicative of a firm with adequate processes and controls	Guidance – indicative of a firm with below adequate processes and controls that may lead to a qualification
3.8 Failure to account Have you seen evidence of firms failing to return client money at the end of the matter? *Rule 14.3 and rule 14.4*	Residual client balances should be returned to clients at the end of a matter. Where this is not possible, there is clear documentation retained which supports the efforts made to return residual client balances.	• Test the exception report of residual client balances to check that the firm has complied with the Rules. • If no exception report exists, obtain a listing of client matters where no time has been charged for at least 90 days and assess if residual client balances exist and the firm has complied with the Rules.	Residual client balances are always returned to clients at the end of a matter and, thus, residual client balances at any one time are rare.	Residual client balances are returned to clients, although, this can take up to 90 days. Residual client balances do exist at any one time; however, the finance team are aware of all of these and are in the process of returning the funds or of dealing with them in accordance with Rules 20.1 (k) and/or Rule 20.2.	• The firm has no effective system in place for complying with Rules 14.3 and 14.4. • Significant – either in themselves or cumulatively – residual client balances are common and the firm cannot therefore return them to clients

Outcome of Reporting Accountant test procedures	General guidance	Examples of areas of focus	Guidance – indicative of firm with above adequate processes and procedures	Guidance – indicative of a firm with adequate processes and controls	Guidance – indicative of a firm with below adequate processes and controls that may lead to a qualification
3.9 Suspense ledgers Have you seen evidence of inappropriate use of a client suspense account? *Rule 29.25*	Where suspense accounts are used, this should be for temporary items only such as an unidentified receipt or payment.	• Identify if suspense accounts are used (recognising that they may be called alternative names such as miscellaneous or in the names of the Partners) • Test the balances outstanding to check that they were posted for good reason and, if they are longstanding, that there has been appropriate review/challenge and an effective plan in place for their closure.	Where suspense accounts are used, items are usually no more than 5 working days old.	Where a suspense account is used, items are usually no more than 30 working days old.	• Widespread unjustified use of suspense accounts. • No process for clearing suspense accounts or outstanding items not followed up.

EXEMPTION TO THE REQUIREMENT TO OBTAIN AN ACCOUNTANT'S REPORT

Please note: This guidance is applicable if your next accounting period end date is **on or after 1 November 2015**.

Status

Whilst this document does not form part of the SRA Handbook, the SRA may have regard to it when exercising its regulatory functions.

Purpose of this guidance

To inform the profession of changes to the SRA Accounts Rules 2011 which allows for an exemption to the requirement to obtain an accountant's report where certain criteria are met and to provide guidance on how to assess whether that criteria has been met.

Relevant rules and law

Rule 32(i) of the SRA Accounts Rules 2011

Firms that hold client monies are required to obtain an accountant's report within 6 months of the end of the period to which the report relates. The report should only be delivered to us if it is **qualified**.

Any firm which holds money for legal aid only will not be required to obtain a report.

Please note you should always deliver an accountant's report regardless of its qualification if you are required to under conditions stated on your practising certificate/firm license or if your firm has ceased handling client money and you are delivering a final report under Rule 33.5.

Changes effective from 1 November 2015

From **1 November 2015**, some firms will be exempt from the requirement to obtain an accountant's report.

The exemption will apply where during the accounting period the average balance on client account does not exceed £10,000 and the maximum in each balance does not exceed £250,000.

During the accounting period a firm must carry out reconciliations of the statement or passbook balance of the general client account and associated accounts. These reconciliations must be carried out, as a minimum, at least once every five weeks. Based on the multiple reconciliations taken over the accounting period the firm must establish (a) the average client money balance (calculated by taking the sum of all reconciliation balances and dividing this by the number of reconciliations) and (b) the maximum of these reconciliation balances. If, based on these balances, your firm satisfies both of the exemption criteria, you will not be required to obtain an accountant's report, unless otherwise required by us (under Rule 32.2) or the firm is ceasing to hold client money, in which case a final report will be required .

Details of how to calculate whether your firm is exempt can be found within the examples below.

Note that the exemption will only apply for accounting periods ending from 1 November 2015 onwards. If your last accounting period ended before that date then you must obtain a report in relation to that period in the usual way.

The exemption will only apply to that accounting period, for example, your firm may be exempt in year 1 as it meets the criteria but not in year 2. It is your firm's responsibility in all cases to make sure that the rules are complied with and if an accountant's report is required, that the report is obtained.

Example 1

The accounting year for Firm A runs from 1 April 2015 to 31 March 2016. The firm undertakes reconciliations at the end of each calendar month:

Reconciliation number	Reconciliation date	Client money balance (including all applicable accounts)
1	30/04/2015	£11,214
2	31/05/2015	£7,487
3	30/06/2015	£9,107
4	31/07/2015	£9,255
5	31/08/2015	£11,394
6	30/09/2015	£9,947
7	31/10/2015	£11,959
8	30/11/2015	£10,053
9	31/12/2015	£8,255
10	31/01/2016	£4,681
11	29/02/2016	£11,105
12	31/03/2016	£7,988

Average balance

Add together the individual reconciliation totals. Total equals £112,445. Divide total by number of reconciliations to obtain average balance. Average equals £112,445 / 12 = £9,370.

Maximum balance

Establish the highest balance from all reconciliations taken. The highest balance from the 12 reconciliations = £11,959.

Test against exemption criteria

Is average balance below £10,000? Yes, average balance = £9,370. Is maximum balance below £250,000? Yes, maximum balance = £11,959.

As both criteria are met the firm is exempt from submitting an accountant's report.

Example 2

The accounting year for Firm B runs from 1 January 2015 to 31 December 2015. The firm undertakes reconciliations once every four weeks (28 days):

Reconciliation number	Reconciliation date	Client money balance (including all applicable accounts)
1	01/01/2015	£23,172
2	29/01/2015	£124,891
3	26/02/2015	£18,184
4	26/03/2015	£10,634
5	23/04/2015	£2,686
6	21/05/2015	£2,209
7	18/06/2015	£654
8	16/07/2015	£19,277
9	13/08/2015	£7,260
10	10/09/2015	£12,016
11	08/10/2015	£21,391
12	05/11/2015	£4,121
13	03/12/2015	£7,107
14	31/12/2015	£8,347

Average balance

Add together the individual reconciliation totals. Total equals £261,949. Divide total by number of reconciliations to obtain average balance. Average equals £261,949 / 14 = £18,711.

Maximum balance

Establish the highest balance from all reconciliations taken. The highest balance from the 14 reconciliations = £124,891.

Test against exemption criteria

Is average balance below £10,000? No, average balance = £18,711. Is maximum balance below £250,000? Yes, maximum balance = £124,891.

As both criteria have not been met, the exemption does not apply and an accountant's report must be obtained.

> It should be noted that where a firm has an accounting year that runs for 18 months then totals should be averaged accordingly (divided by 18). The same principle applies to where the firm carry out a weekly reconciliation.

How should I submit my accountant's report?

You should submit your report by email to the Accountant's report team.[2] You will receive an automated response confirming receipt which you will be able to retain as proof of delivery.

If you wish to send the report by post,[3] we recommend a tracked service such as recorded/special delivery.

Where can I find a copy of the AR1 form?

You can download a copy of the AR1 Accountant's Report form on this page (see top of the page).

When will my report be due?

You must obtain your accountant's report within six months of your firm's accounting period end date.

For example, if your accounting period ends on 31 December 2015, you must obtain the report by the deadline of 30 June 2016.

If the report is qualified it also must be submitted to us by that deadline.

If for any reason your accounting period should change, you must notify us without delay as the reporting deadline will also change accordingly.

This is my first report, what will my accounting period be?

The accounting period must commence from the exact date on which client money was first held by your firm.

When we receive notification of this date, a standard twelve month accounting period will be set up on our system.

Although the report may be submitted to us by the accountant, the responsibility for ensuring that it is delivered rests with you and your firm.

Can I change my accounting period?

Yes, you can make a request to change your accounting period. Written requests must be received before the reporting deadline in order to be considered. Firms can have an accounting period of less than 12 months or up to a maximum of 18 months.

I am unable to obtain my Accountant's report on time, can I apply for an extension?

Yes, if you are unable to meet the reporting deadline, you can apply for an extension of time to obtain the report. Extensions can be granted for a period of up to 3 months at this office. Requests can only be considered if received before the reporting deadline.

2. Email **sraaccountantsreports@sra.org.uk**.
3. See **7.1** for SRA contact details.

Can I apply for a waiver?

Yes, applications for waivers from the need to obtain an accountant's report should be made to the Accountant's report team. Where appropriate, firms may be granted a waiver of the obligation to obtain an accountant's report. It is the responsibility of the firm to demonstrate exceptional circumstances in order for a waiver to be considered.

What happens if I obtain and/or deliver a qualified report late?

If your firm's report is required to be delivered to the SRA and is received late, it will be treated as a late submission. The provisions of Regulation 3.1(c) of the SRA Practising Regulations 2011 will apply.

This means that you and any individuals who are responsible for the obtaining and delivery of the report will be required to pay an additional fee of £200 when applying for your next practising certificate.

You will not be included in the organisation's bulk renewal application and will be required to make an individual application. This will be available in the My services section of your mySRA account.

My firm is changing legal status, what are my reporting requirements under these circumstances?

If your firm is changing legal status, we will require separate accountant's reports for both entities.

> For example:
>
> A firm changing from a sole practice to a partnership on 30 September 2014.

In these circumstances, you are required to provide a final accountant's report for the sole practice up to the exact date on which the firm held client money as a sole practice, in this case 30 September 2014.

The firm would then be required to obtain their first report as a partnership, for the period from 1 October 2014 onwards.

I have not held any client money, do I still need to deliver a report?

No, in accordance with Rule 32.1 of the Accounts Rules, if you have not held client money for the relevant accounting period, you will not be required to deliver an accountants' report.

Should you begin holding client money at any time in the future, the obligation to obtain an accountant's reports will apply from that date, unless the firm is exempt.

If you have any queries on the SRA Accounts Rules, contact the Professional Ethics Guidance Team.[4]

4. See **7.1** for contact details.

[7] Further sources of information and support

[7.1] Useful contacts

Law Society

- The **Practice Advice Service** provides support for solicitors on a wide range of areas of practice, and can be contacted on 020 7320 5675 from 09.00 to 17.00 on weekdays.
- **Law Society Risk and Compliance Advisory Service** offers expert and confidential support and guidance, including face-to-face consultancy on risk and compliance and finance and accounting: telephone 020 7316 5655, or email **consulting@lawsociety.org.uk**.
- **Lawyerline** gives advice to solicitors on client care and complaints handling: telephone 020 7320 5720 or email **lawyerline@lawsociety.org.uk**.

See **www.lawsociety.org.uk**.

SRA

- **Contact Centre:** telephone 0370 606 2555 (+44 (0)121 329 6800 for international callers) from 08.00 to 18.00 on Mondays, Wednesdays, Thursdays and Fridays, and from 09.30 to 18.00 on Tuesdays.
- **Professional Ethics Helpline:** telephone 0370 606 2577 between 09.00 and 17.00 on weekdays, or email **professional.ethics@sra.org.uk**.

See **www.sra.org.uk**.

Other membership organisations

- Association of Chartered Certified Accountants (ACCA) (**www.accaglobal.com**).
- ACCA Members' Advisory (email advisory@accaglobal.com; **www.accaglobal.com/uk/en/technical-activities.html**).
- Institute of Chartered Accountants in England and Wales (ICAEW) (**www.icaew.com**)
- ICAEW Solicitors Group (telephone 01908 248 250; email **sigs@icaew.com**).
- Institute of Legal Finance and Management (ILFM) – education authority and membership body for legal finance, administration and practice management professionals (**www.ilfm.org.uk**).

[7.2] Useful publications

Law Society

- **Law Society newsletters** – a number of different newsletters and e-bulletins are produced, including Professional Update and Anti-Money Laundering Update: visit the Law Society website to subscribe.
- *Legal Compliance Bulletin* – produced by the Law Society to provide up-to-date, practical information on every aspect of legal compliance and regulation for solicitors, barristers and practice managers: visit the Law Society website to subscribe.

SRA

- **SRA Update** – an e-newsletter sent to all regulated individuals but others can subscribe by e-mailing a subscription request to **SRAupdate@sra.org.uk**.
- **SRA's Compliance News** – an e-newsletter sent automatically to COLPs and COFAs, but others can sign up to the mailing list: search Compliance News on the SRA website to subscribe.

Index to the SRA Accounts Rules 2011

[This index is based on a version published in the Solicitors' Accounts Rules 2008, updated for this 14th edition of the Solicitors' Accounts Manual to cover the changes arising from the introduction of the SRA Accounts Rules 2011, as amended from October 2011 to November 2016 inclusive, and incorporating a few corrections in the order of entries.] This index does not form part of the Rules. References are to the numbers of the Rules. An 'n' after the Rule number refers to one of the non-mandatory guidance notes appended to that Rule. References to the appendices are prefaced by 'app'.